Customary International Law

A Comprehensive Study of State Practice, Opinio Juris, and the Legitimacy of Norm Formation

Charles Quince

Series in Law

Vernon Press

www.vernonpress.com

In the Americas:

Vernon Press
1000 N West Street, Suite 1200,
Wilmington, Delaware 19801
United States

In the rest of the world:

Vernon Press
C/Sancti Espiritu 17,
Malaga, 29006
Spain

Series in Law

ISBN: 979-8-8819-0424-1

Cover design by Vernon Press. Image by maylim on Freepik.

Table of Contents

Introduction ix
Disclaimer x

Chapter I
The International and Geopolitical Systems 1
The International System and the International Legal System 3

Chapter II
Article 38 of the Statute of the Permanent Court of International Justice 5
Historical Background 5
Analysis of the Committee 8
Doctrinal Interpretations 10

Chapter III
State Consent and International Customary Law 13
Value-Oriented Customary International Law 13
The Need for State Consent 15
Consent and Compliance 15
The Legitimacy of Consent 17
Consent as a Protective Shield 18
The Theoretical Framework of State Consent 19
Analysis of Consensualist Theories 19
The Autolimitation Theory 19
The Theory of Collective Will 22
State Consent and the Legitimate Authority of Customary International Law 23
Challenges and Perplexities Concerning State Consent 24
Complications of State Consent 25
The Merits of State Consent 26
State Consent as a Barrier Against Domination 27
The Predictability of State Consent 27
State Consent and Status Equality 28

Chapter IV
State Practice 29

An Overview of National Digests and the Concept of State Practice 29
The Council of European Resolutions 29
Repertoire de la pratique française enmatière de droit international public 30
Repertório of the Brazilian Practice of Public International Law 30
Swiss Directory of Public International Law 30
Italian Practice of International Law 31
The Digest of United States Practice of International Law 31
The Australian Yearbook of International Law 32
The Japanese Annual of International Law 32
The Canadian Yearbook of International Law 32
Documents on Swedish Foreign Policy 32
The South Africa Yearbook of International Law 33
The British Digest of International Law 33
An Examination of Case Law 33
Notable International Law Cases 34
The *Asylum Case* 34
Right of Passage Case 34
US Nationals in Morocco 34
The North Sea Continental Shelf Cases 34
Nuclear Tests Case 35
State Entities and the International Legal System 35
Evidence of Customary International Law 36
Role of Non-State Entities 37
State Responsibility and the Customary Process 37
Position of State Organs in the Customary Process 38
State Practice and *Opinio Juris* 38
Challenges to Broader Notions of State Practice 39
Claims and Declarations in State Practice 40
Physical Assertion vs. Claims 40
Limitations of Physical Assertion Emphasis 41
The Scope of International Practice and Types of Custom 43
Requirements for Different Types of Custom 43

General Custom and the Question of Generality 44
Binding Nature and Derogation from General Customary Rules 45
Lex Specialis Derogat Legi Generali 46
The Principle as a General Principle of Law 46
Practical Issues and Limitations 47
Universal and General Custom 48
Normative Enhancement of Customary Rules 49
Customary International Law: Formation and Objection 49
General Uniformity 49
Individual Consistency 51
Continuity and Repetition 52
The Persistent Objector: Historical Background 53
The Persistent Objector and Original Consent 55
Original Consent as a Foundation for Universalism 55
Original Consent Challenging the Persistent Objector Doctrine 56
The Problem of Foreseeability in Customary International Law 56
Treaties, Customary International Law, and the Persistent Objector 57
The Persistent Objector: Further Analysis 57
The *Fisheries* Case 58
The *Asylum* Case 59
Limitations of the Persistent Objector Doctrine 60
Case Studies: France and South Africa 61
The Role of General Acquiescence 61
Implications and Conclusions 62
Chapter V
The Subjective Element 65
Theories Related to an Established Customary Rule 65
The Court and Case Law 65
1. The Subjective Element as a Belief in a Set of Legal Correlatives 65
2. The Subjective Element as a Belief in Legal Duty/ Obligation 66
3. The Subjective Element as a Belief in a Legal Right 66

4. The Subjective Element as a Recognition of the Validity of a Rule in Conventional and Customary International Law 66
5. The Subjective Element as the Opinion on the Content of a Customary Rule 67
6. The Subjective Element as a Factor That Determines Legally Relevant Omissions 67
7. The Subjective Element as the Expression of Acceptance of a Customary Rule 67
8. The Subjective Element as a Recognition of a Customary Rule 68
Analysis of the Court's Formulations 68
Evolutionary Developments in Customary International Law 75
Theoretical Frameworks on the Subjective Element 75
Critical Analysis of Cheng's Examples 76
Alternative Perspective on Cheng's Framework 77
D'Amato's Claim-Oriented Perspective 77
Critiques of D'Amato's Theory 78
Thirlway's Perspective: Opinio Necessitatis 79
Social Necessity and the Law 79
The Pre-Existing Rule School 80
The Relationship between the Subjective Element and State Practice 81
The Subjective Element by Another Name? 81

Chapter VI
The Customary Process: A Theoretical and Practical Examination 85
State Actions and the International System 85
Social Factors and State Behavior 85
Expectations 86
State Preferences and Interactions in International Relations 87
Preferences 87
The Role of Attributes in Interactions 87
Structural Effects 88
Differentiated Values for Behaviors 88
Decentralized Interactions 88
Behavior Determinants and the Formation of Rules 89

The Legal Influence of State Acts and Interactions 90
State Acts and Legal Relationships 91
The Concept of Legal Claims and the Customary Process 91
The Development of Legal Relationships 93
Negative Acts, Recognition, and Renunciation 94
Positive Acts, Recognition, and Renunciation 96
Types of Recognition and Adoption 96
1. Recognition without Adoption 96
2. Recognition with Adoption 97
Coordinated Recognition 98
Impediments to Legal Relationships 98
Requirements for Diplomatic Protests 99
Effectiveness of Diplomatic Protests 99
Countermeasures Beyond Protests 100
Compromises and Their Effects 100
Effects of the General State of the Law 101
International Organizations 102
Identification and Definition of Customary Rules 102
The Development of Customary Rules 107
The Codification and Development of International Law 110
The Importance of Law-Making Procedures 110
Codifying Conferences and Conventions 112

Chapter VII
The Development of Customary International Law and the Two-Hundred-Mile EEZ 113
Widespread and Consistent State Practice 113
The Package Deal Argument 115
Repetition of the Practice over a Considerable Time Period 116
Opinio Juris 117
Rejection and Acceptance 117
The Scope of the EEZ Concept in Customary International Law 119
National Practice 119
Recent Jurisprudence of the ICJ 120
The Exclusive Economic Zone and Customary International Law 123
The High Seas 124
Submarine Cables 126

The Regime of Islands 126
Landlocked and Geographically Disadvantaged States 126
Marine Pollution 127
Marine Scientific Research 128

Table of Cases 129

Endnotes by Chapter 131

Bibliography 167

Index 171

Introduction

Customary international law is one of the most recognized sources of international law. Its decline as a law-making mechanism has, to paraphrase Mark Twain, been greatly exaggerated.[1] The norm development efforts of the United Nations have facilitated the creation of customary law on the international level. However, the concept of customary international law is subject to controversial and complex debates that call for the need to examine it in great detail.

This study involves two central objectives:

1. To clarify the intricate nature that defines customary international law, addressing it both as a law-creating mechanism and as a perceptible body of international rules
2. To develop a methodology through which a custom norm can be identified

The first six chapters will analyze the following questions:

- What is the relationship between the international system as a whole and the international legal system, and how does the geo-political process influence this relationship?
- What is State consent and its function within the norm development process?
- What is *opinion juris sive necessitatis* and its capacity within the development of customary international law?
- What is the role of State practice, what entities of the State are represented by it, and what are the requirements for it?
- How does the development of custom function?

Scholars and commentators have discussed, at length, the queries that are posed above. However, an examination of the various debates and discourses on the customary doctrine leaves far too many questions than it does answers. As this study progresses, we will see how some studies show logical inconsistency, others misinterpret the interrelationship between State practice and inter-State relations, while others simply provide an incomplete analysis of the whole customary international law process.

How does this study fit within the paradigm of examining customary international law? First, it is by no means definitive, nor is it an exhaustive study of the subject at hand. I will attempt to address the theoretical difficulties associated with the concept of customary international law and see if they can be resolved within the parameters of State practice. While this study seeks to provide tentative answers, it also seeks to raise other questions and debates for further examination.

Concerning methodology, this work consists of seven chapters:

- Chapter I explores the international and geopolitical systems
- Chapter II analyzes Article 38 of the Statute of the Permanent Court of International Justice
- Chapter III examines State consent
- Chapter IV covers State practice
- Chapter V investigates the subjective element of customary international law
- Chapter VI deals with the theoretical inner workings of the customary process
- Chapter VII covers the relationship between customary international law and the two-hundred-mile Exclusive Economic Zone

This methodology will not only show the uniqueness of the topics concerning customary international law but also how each topical subject is connected to the whole. This structure is designed to give a comprehensive review of the main issues regarding customary international law and may compel the reader to explore this complex subject further.

Disclaimer

Certain chapters in this book (Chapters 3, 4, 5, and 6) were edited using AI tools to assist with grammar and syntax correction. All final content has been reviewed by the author to ensure accuracy and consistency in tone and style.

Chapter I
The International and Geopolitical Systems

The international and geopolitical systems generally refer to the constellations of States that interact with each other on the global level. Theoretically, the systemic approach to these global relations is defined by: the presence of collaborative actions between nation-states or elements; the integration of these cooperative interactions into a whole; and the fact that the whole does not correlate with the sum of its elements. The existence of these components on the global level is a definitive representation of the international system.[1]

The concept of interdependence is also an integral part of the international system. Collaborative actions and interactions are underlying attributes of this system. But what exactly is interdependence? On the most fundamental level, it is a structural feature of the international system and involves interconnection among actors on the global level.[2] Yet, on a deeper level, interdependence goes far beyond the definition of interconnectedness. It implies a relationship in which various parties are associated in such a way that changes in one party invariably alter the outcomes or objectives of another.[3] Some commentators suggest that interdependence is not only an essential part of the international system, but is on a compatible level with anarchy.[4] In short, they are different characteristics within the international system in which two actors measure their relationship and their independence.[5] Generally, this analysis comes under the rubric of strategic interdependence, which involves a subjective choice made by one of the participants and under structural interdependence, which consists of an examination of the relationship itself.[6] Under the concept of strategic independence, each actor faces repercussions for violating their obligations.[7]

Two prevailing elements organize the international system: (1) the hierarchical structure of the system's units, and (2) the distribution of the units according to their unique capabilities.[8] The hierarchy principle, the factor that determines how various units fit within the system according to their capabilities, is anarchy. Anarchy is essentially the absence of a centralized world government and the existence of a decentralized palatinate where its unit is autonomous when it comes to any decision-making process.[9] Whether any type of standard order is feasible depends on the subjectivity of the individual. Some commentators suggest that the international order is defined as a pattern of activity that sustains or facilitates the fundamental objectives of States on the global level.[10]

Thus, from this perspective, the international system may be anarchic and still represents some type of order among nations.

As mentioned above, the structure of the international system is determined by the distribution of the capabilities that exist among units within the system. On the global level, capabilities are unevenly divided among the various units, which explains the de facto system of stratification that often characterizes an oligarchic structure of power. The chief units within the global system are States. Their roles are generally predicated on self-preservation and increasing their own capabilities. In short, each unit in the international system participates in a global competition for ways to increase its own power.[11] Cooperative efforts between the various units generally revolve around the perceptions of common interests and the accommodation of these interests.[12]

The international system works under the basic premise that mutually affected units contribute to the legal and political dynamics of the system. In essence, the structure of the system is a contributing factor to how the units behave and the outcome of their behavior. While a unit may not control the legal-politico process that occurs within the system, its behavior can result in unwanted consequences that result from structural impediments.[13] The structure of the international system has a defining influence on the way units behave. For example, the asymmetric distribution of capabilities suggests that more wealthy and powerful States play a prominent role within the international system. According to this hierarchical system, these powerful States' influence is predicated on the reaction or behavior of other States within the system.[14] The systemic structure of various units that have different capabilities facilitates intrastate competition. When there is competitiveness among units that are both interdependent and autonomous, individual initiative on the part of the units is unpredictable because their actions depend upon the behavior of other units.[15]

Some commentators suggest that the international system should be organized on the social character.[16] In other words, the global system is more comparable when its units are structured according to the same values and principles. Applying this perspective to the modern international system, we find that the units are analogous to each other. However, upon further examination, we also see traces of both uniformity and comparability among contemporary units. For example, if we keep in mind the common interests and objectives displayed by States when it comes to securing peace and security, the system is uniform. However, each unit has its own domestic interests and objectives, and the resources they have to achieve their aims vary accordingly. In some instances, States may act in a uniform fashion to achieve their objectives and may oppose other nations if their interests impede these efforts. All these collateral influences indicate the comparability of the international system.

The International System and the International Legal System

The structural formation of the international legal system mirrors the international system. In short, when taking into consideration the anarchic structure of the international system, international law supports the notion that each State has sovereign equality, and the relationships between States are based on collaboration and amalgamation.[17] The prevailing ordering principle of the international system highlights the point that, unlike the domestic system, the international system does not have a centralized legislative organ, a judicial entity with compulsory powers, nor a centralized authority that is empowered to enforce the decisions of the judicial organ.[18] Its institutional substructure is composed of decentralized law-creating mechanisms, which are voluntary in nature when it comes to settling disputes and enforcing international norms. The rules associated with international law are predicated on the conditional consent of those it applies to.[19]

The concept of decentralization as it applies to the international system does not mean that each unit of the system is an autonomous and self-sufficient legislative authority. Similar to the domestic sphere, the international sphere is a social construct. Some scholars understand that the legal system places inherent restrictions on individual freedom, which compels other individuals to form cooperative relationships that ultimately determine the consequences of individuals' behavior.[20] This assertion represents the international legal system because this type of relationship generally creates the general norms of international law, which attempts to bring some order to the global community. In international legal discourse, the disorganized ensemble of units is generally expressed in terms of the *international community of States.*[21] Therefore, Article 53 of the Vienna Convention on the Law of Treaties prescribes that a particular international norm is a rule of *jus cogens* only if it is accepted as such by the international community of States as a whole.[22]

International law and international institutions are the very foundation of the international system. International law justifies the international system by utilizing a set of fundamental norms and principles which is required to maintain peace and order within the international system. For example, the principle of equity among the States, along with the concepts of territorial integrity and political independence, is attained through the uniform and universal implementation of rules. These concepts contribute to what is commonly referred to as the public policy of the international community.[23]

International law can be considered a foundational structure that determines not only the international system's structure but also a defining element when it comes to constraining the actions of States.[24] Every State is obligated to accept some degree of legal restraint on its own autonomy and independence if it is to be a functional component of the international system. However, the role that international law plays goes far beyond restricting the actions of States; it also regulates and determines the consequences for States that violate international norms.[25] Without international law as a defining anchor, the process of ensuring peace and security on the global level would be very difficult. International law ensures that States have both rights and duties, which are needed to define them as subjects of international law.[26]

There seems to be an imbalance between the need to strengthen the international system and the struggle for power among States.[27] This swaying between cooperative efforts and conflict within the international system influences the corpus of international law. Generally, any form of international regulatory actions inherently contains a certain degree of cooperation, but there must be a clear distinction between patterns of cooperation and patterns of conflict on the global level. Cooperative efforts are generally associated with systemic rules and norms of international law, which are community-oriented in expression but differ from primary rules because they are not imperative when it comes to the sustainment of the international system.[28] Homogeneity seems to be the defining factor when it comes to applying the general rules and principles of international law. This is also important when ascertaining a pattern of structural relations that exist amongst the norms of the international legal system. When it comes to conflicts, they usually arise when States place emphasis on their own foreign policy objectives. These actions generally facilitate competitive environments that not only cause fragmentation in legal regimes but also impact the effectiveness of international norms.[29] The degree of this conflict can be seen in mechanisms or techniques whereby States may avoid or alter specific rules in order to have specific norms accommodate their interests. Reservations and compromise texts contained within the body of treaties are good examples of this.

Chapter II
Article 38 of the Statute of the Permanent Court of International Justice

Historical Background

The Permanent Court of International Justice evolved as an entity by Article 14 of the Covenant of the League of Nations. A planning committee, the Advisory Committee of Jurists, was established to develop a Statute for the fledgling organization.[1] During the initial stages of the planning Committee, the States presented various plans for the constitution of the Court. Some of the suggestions by the States made no reference to the rules that would be applicable to the Courts, while other States presented a detailed, enumerated list for review.

In 1918, Denmark, Norway, and Sweden presented a draft for an international juridical organization that would apply, in the absence of any conventional law, established rules of international law or generally recognized rules.[2] This initial plan was eventually replaced by the Five Neutral Powers plan developed by Denmark, the Netherlands, Norway, Sweden, and Switzerland, which called for the application of general recognized rules of international law in the absence of any treaty provisions.[3] Switzerland suggested that the Court apply the generally recognized rules of the laws of nations in the absence of any agreements.[4] Germany also presented an alternative plan, which stated that the Court should decide issues in accordance with international agreements, customary international law, and the general principles of law and equity.[5] In addition to these recommendations, the Committee entertained plans put forth by the Interparliamentary Union and the International Law Union. Other instruments, such as the Convention for the Establishment of a Central American Court of Justice, outlined points of law that the Court should consider that correlate to the principles of international law.[6]

After reviewing the recommendations, Lord Phillimore supported the language highlighted in the Five Powers' project with minor changes. He wanted to add to the language '*rules of international law*' and the words '*from whatever source they may be derived*' in order to clarify the Court's application of customary international law.[7] Even though the Final Report of the Committee mentioned and praised the Five Powers plan, the Committee only implemented various aspects of the plan. The first text that the Committee considered was the suggestion made by Baron Descamps, which stated that the judges of the Court should resolve international disputes by ascertaining:

1. Conventional international law, both general and specific, as expressed by the States;
2. Customary international law, with the State practice being done out of a sense of legal obligation;
3. Rules of international law as recognized by civilized nations; and
4. International jurisprudence as a means for applying and developing international law.[8]

Descamps' suggestion represents some of the same outlines that are common to most of the proposals stated above. First, there is a notion of precedence when it comes to applying the various rules of international law. Secondly, although it is ambiguous when it comes to a clear definition, customary international law is treated as a distinct category of international law. Descamps' recommendations were eventually replaced by the proposals submitted by Elihu Root and Lord Phillimore. Their proposals stated that the Court should consider:

1. General and specific international law and rules expressly adopted by States which are party to a dispute;
2. Customary international law, being recognized practice performed out of a sense of legal obligation;
3. General principles of law recognized by civilized countries; and
4. Judicial decisions and the opinions of writers as a means for the application and development of law.[9]

The word *recognized* became a part of the English version in the second point of this new proposal. The French wording of the text retained the words *pratique commune* (common practice), which added a sense of ambiguity to the provision during interpretation. This modification was repudiated by a later proposal sponsored by Baron Descamps and Lord Phillimore, and amended by Rucci-Busatti. This proposal stated that the Court should settle disputes by:

1. International conventions, either general or specific, as constituting rules expressly adopted by the States which are party to the dispute;
2. International custom as evidence of common practice of States, accepted by them as law;
3. The general principles of law recognized by civilized nations.

The Court should also consider judicial decisions rendered by analogous cases, and the opinions of the best-qualified writers.[10]

This version of the proposal solidified the correlation between the English and French texts and added one major significance: customary rules, for the purpose of widespread application, should be in force between the parties to the dispute. In other words, the parties should follow a particular practice out of a sense of legal obligation.

During the twenty-fourth meeting of the Committee, Lord Phillimore and Elihu Root put forth various issues that needed attention. The Root-Phillimore proposal discarded the modification of the second point suggested in the last plan but preserved the fundamental features of the previous proposals. Article 31 of this plan stated that the Court should settle disputes by applying:

1. Conventional international law, whether general or special, forming the rules expressing adopted by the States which are parties to the case;
2. International custom, as evidence of a common practice in use between nations and accepted by them as law;
3. The general principles of law recognized by civilized countries; and
4. The precedent of judicial decisions and the opinions of the publicists as means for the application and development of law.[11]

Subsequently, a Draft Committee was created to organize the existing proposals into a single draft. The Committee put forth guidelines of how the Court was to apply the rules. The second point mirrored the earlier text versions, and the final Draft stated that the Court shall, within its jurisdiction as expressed in Article 34, apply:

1. International conventions, whether general or particular, establishing rules expressly recognized by the contesting States;
2. International custom, as evidence of a general practice, which is performed out of a sense of legal obligation;
3. The general principles of law recognized by civilized nations; and
4. Judicial decisions and the teachings of the most highly qualified publicists of various nations, as subsidiary means of ascertaining the rules of law.[12]

The second paragraph of the Draft Scheme was accepted without reservations when reviewed by the Council and the Third Committee of the League of Nations. The only country that suggested any type of modifications was Argentina. The Argentinian plan stated that the Court should consider: (2) International custom, as evidence of a practice founded on principles of justice and humanity, and accepted as law.[13]

The Third Committee rejected Argentina's modifications and accepted paragraph two as it was expressed in the Draft Scheme of the Advisory Committee of Jurists.[14] The final version of the Draft Scheme presented to the First Assembly of the League of Nations by the Third Committee stated:

Article 38. The Court should apply:

1. International conventions, whether general or particular, establishing rules expressly recognized by the contesting States;
2. International custom, as evidence of a general practice accepted as law;
3. The general principles of law recognized by civilized nations; and
4. Subject to the provisions of art. 59, judicial decisions and teachings of the most highly qualified publicists of the various nations, as subsidiary means for the determination of rules of law;

This provision shall not prejudice the power of the Court to decide a case *ex aequo et bono*, if the parties agree thereto.[15] In December 1920, this version of the Final Draft Scheme was approved by the Assembly of the League of Nations in a Resolution concerning the establishment of the Permanent Court of International Justice.[16] An examination of the Statute was conducted in 1929 by another Committee of Jurists, but Article 38 remained virtually the same, except for a minor modification added in paragraph four of the French text.[17]

Analysis of the Committee

Were the debates surrounding the various plans united by a singular voice? There is no solid answer to this question. Examining the article and how it evolved does not address this query in its full context because the final draft of this article contains modifications and compromises of different legal traditions.[18] Additionally, just because certain members of the Committee agreed on particular aspects during the developmental stages of the article does not mean that they were united on the subject during the interpretative stage. Lack of sufficient records of the proceedings in their entirety makes it very hard to ascertain the opinions of the members concerning various proposals. In spite of this, we can still gain some perspective on the thought process of the Committee members.

In clarifying his proposal, Baron Descamps judicious stated that an established custom is a rule established by the continual and general usage by nations, which has therefore attained the status of law. Custom, he noted, resulted from the belief in a legal obligation and the need for this obligation to facilitate intrastate relations.[19] The repetition element is highlighted in his definition when he used the term *continual*, and his reference to 'general usage' seems to indicate that he was only concern with general customary international law. The one outstanding feature of Descamps' exposition is that he considers the force of law as a side effect of the elements of repetition and generality of practice. If he really felt that the force of law was essentially a mere consequence, then it is reasonable to believe that the determinant factor for the development of a customary norm is the existence of a general practice and that the practice is performed out of a sense of legal obligation.

Examining Descamps' proposal highlights the similarities it has with Isidore's definition of customary international law: "custom is a kind of law instituted by general conduct, which is accepted as law [i.e., written law] when law is lacking."[20] The definition of custom given by Suarez correlates with Descamps' interpretation of the term. Suarez suggests that the expression accepted by law specifies the juridical element of customary international law and that the repetition of general conduct is emblematic of the concept of custom.[21]

Was the concept of practice done out of a sense of legal obligation a widespread notion among the members of the Committee? Four members of the Committee supported the notion that practice done out of a sense of legal obligation was valid. These members were Root, Loder, Lord Phillimore, and de Lapradelle.[22] The Final Report of the Committee, in reference to the rules that the Court should analyze when adjudicating issues, noted that customary international law's continuity is evidence of common practice, which correlates to the element of practice done out of a sense of legal obligation.[23] There could be an assertion that the Committee regarded the term *accepted as law* as referring to the normative quality of the customary rule or to the consent of the States to the corresponding rule. Rucci-Busatti was the only member who opposed the expression contained in paragraph two.

Rucci-Busatti suggested that customary international law could only be applied by the Court if the parties involved in the dispute followed a specific practice and did so out of a sense of legal obligation. This perspective supports the notion that the rule be recognized as a binding force on each party, which equates customary law with treaty law. It is not very hard to see why he stated that "custom, like any other convention applicable to a case, must be in force between the parties in dispute."[24] Two of his contemporaries, Henry Bonfils and Paul Fauchille, agreed with his suggestion. They asserted that reciprocity was an important element in the development of customary international law because custom implied binding obligations.[25] Whether the Committee rejected Rucci-Busatti's proposal because it highlighted custom as a rule applicable to States is debatable. The most likely reason that the Committee rejected his view is that the Court may possibly apply a custom rule to a State without first establishing that the rule was recognized by the State.

The definition of customary rules as recognized rules is a recurring theme in the proposals submitted by the States. Exactly what was meant by the term 'recognition' is unclear, since the notes of the proceedings did not provide any explanation. Recognition likely meant the context that Elihu Root or Lord Phillimore put it. Root stated that customary law is *positive international law*, while Lord Phillimore referred to it as international law in practical terms.[26]

Nevertheless, the first amendment supported by Root and Lord Phillimore emphasized that custom would be "recognized practice between nations accepted by them as law." Both Root and Phillimore supported the elimination of the word recognized from the corpus of future texts, which suggests that they both believe that the term added very little to the force of the proposal. Case in point, the Committee might presume that when States take actions which is considered as a matter of law, their actions and conduct implicitly represent the establishment and acknowledgement of customary international law.

One of the most important aspects concerning the amendment to the text involves the second point proposed by Argentina – that practice should be considered principles accepted as law – which was rejected by the Sub-Committee of the Third Committee of the League of Nations. The Argentinian proposal suggested that not all general practices created a customary norm, even if the norm was accepted as law. Why? Because it would limit the effectiveness of States' actions as a law-creating mechanism. Additionally, there are no thresholds to be passed that would ascertain exactly when the participation in a practice becomes customary international law. The rejection of this proposed amendment indicates support for this assertion.

Paragraph two of Article 38 acknowledges the general practice requirement, which seems to imply that the Committee ignored or did not consider the possibility of the Court applying a special customary rule. There are a number of reasons why the Committee adopted the position it did. The Committee perhaps felt that such a rule could not develop; that this type of rule required evidence or proof of its recognition by States before the Court could apply it; or the Committee wanted to catalogue and characterize only specific general rules of international law.

Doctrinal Interpretations

The terminologies associated with Article 38(2) of the Statute of the Permanent Court of International Justice and Article 38(1)(b) of the Statute of the International Court of Justice have been interpreted in various ways. Three specific interpretations have been applied to these provisions. The first centers upon the description of a certain or particular type of customary rule that the Court applies. Another interpretation has to do with the process of how a customary rule is developed. The third interpretation focuses on authorizing the Court to apply a certain type of practice, rather than a legal rule, in disputes.[1] However, the application of the practice is qualified.

There can be clarity to these types of questions if one speculates that Article 38 allows various types of international rules that the Court is compelled to apply, and that paragraph two represents a definitive customary norm. This, however, does not account for the evolution of a customary rule within the legal process. The customary rule to be applied, within the context of Article 38, has already been perfected, which explains why the corresponding practice is considered *lex lata* or accepted as law. There is a very good reason for this: States would be reluctant to allow the Court to apply a customary rule which might be contradicted by another established or fledgling rule which would be opposed by other States.

One of the chief criticisms of Article 38's provisional terminology is that a customary norm, as expressed by the Article, is not evidence of a general practice, but the reverse is true. Within this context, Descamps' original proposal would have been a better composition since it avoided the term *evidence* and used the word *being* which clarified exactly what the definition of custom meant. There's also the contention that the expression "accepted as law" is built upon the notion that customary rules exist prior to the concept of general practice, which means that general practice would be the only evidence of that rule.[2] There is no strong evidence that the members considered this notion of customary law. As previously noted, examination of the positions during the work stages of the Committee seems to suggest that the theoretical framework that the majority of the members supported involved the notion that customary rules result from State practice.

Although Article 38 endured criticisms and subjective interpretations, the PCIJ implemented it with very few problems. When the United Nations Conference on International Organization started its work to develop the International Court of Justice, States recommended two pertinent items concerning the inclusion of this article into the Statute of the future Court. The Informal Inter-Allied Committee supported the preservation of this article by stating that "although the wording of this provision is open to criticism, it has worked well in practice and its retention is recommended." Venezuela stated similar views when it asserted that the provision of Article 38 was not objected to.[3]

The United Nations Committee of Jurists enshrined the text of the article within the corpus of the Statute of the International Court of Justice. The Committee decided to preserve the text on the grounds that the text would cause fewer problems in practice than it would as a stand-alone doctrine. Its Final Report emphasized that it fully expected the future Court to make the text operational as a practical doctrine. The actions of both the PCIJ and the ICJ indicate that neither Court has been limited to a strict interpretation of Article 38, always ready to integrate the developments of State practice and international relations into their decision-making process. By the 1930s, many arbitration treaties had assimilated the Article completely within the provisions of applicable law.[4]

Chapter III
State Consent and International Customary Law

Value-Oriented Customary International Law

It is perfectly understandable to hold the notion that all law, including customary international law, develops from practice: a product of what States actually *do*, where such acts as public pronouncements represent the official stance of a government's policy. Within this context, *opinio juris*, a definitive factor in the development of customary norms, should not be contrasted with the concept of practice. Law is paradigmatically developed through the actions of States. Thus, State practice equates to the creation of laws.

Nonetheless, in seeking to clarify the orthodox understanding of customary international law – according to which custom involves a combination of general State practice and *opinio juris* – we can consider these components as two forms of practice, or two aspects under which practice may be interpreted. In ascertaining whether a putative norm exists within the context of international custom, we begin by giving it some type of form or content (i.e., the geographical parameters of the territorial sea, the immunity of sovereign States from specific kinds of intervention, etc.). This content specifies a particular pattern of State behavior to which normative valence (obligatory, permissible, impermissible, etc.) is assigned under certain circumstances.

To determine whether this legal norm, which will be labelled ***X***, exists as a matter of customary international law, two pertinent questions must be asked, which pertain to State activities bearing on practice and *opinio juris* relevant to custom:

1. **State practice:** Is there sufficient evidence that States generally conform their actions and behavior to ***X***? Do States generally take action or refrain from taking action in accordance with what ***X*** obligates them to do?
2. ***Opinio Juris*:** Is there sufficient evidence that States adopt one or the other following attitudes to ***X***: (A) **OJ1** - The creation of an international legal rule according to the specified pattern of behavior has the normative significance attached to it by ***X*** is ethically justified, and such rule should be created by a process that involves general State practice consistent with ***X***, with the consent of States that abide by ***X***'s legal rule (fig. 1); or (B) **OJ2** - ***X*** is already a customary norm (i.e., it exists as a

matter of general State practice and *opinio juris*) and the compliance with the legal norm of ***X*** is ethically justified. (fig. III.2)

In essence, *opinio juris* involves either the belief that a norm is already a part of customary international law and compliance with it is ethically justified or that it should be established as law through the process of general State practice and *opinio juris*.

An advantage of this syllogistic disjunctive description of *opinio juris* is that it disseminates the ambiguities or the enigma of custom. It does so by highlighting or emphasizing the theoretical framework that posits that the development of new customary norms is inherently premised on the deception on the part of States.[1] Although some commentators have minimized the significance of this enigma, other commentators suggest that it threatens the very legitimacy of customary international law because there is a feasible transparency constraint on any form of law-making. Political legitimacy demands that political power be exercised, including acts of law-making.

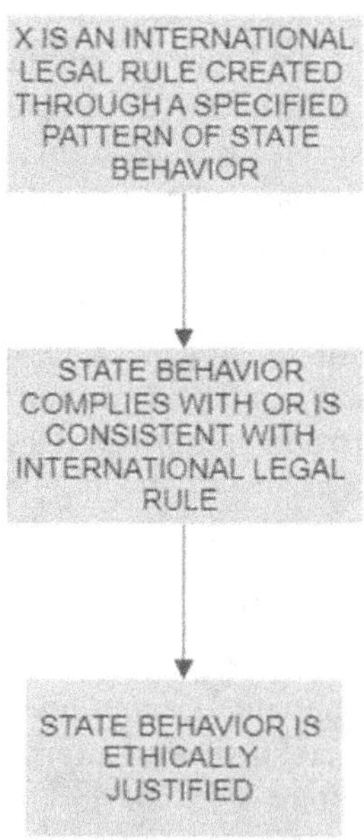

Figure III.1

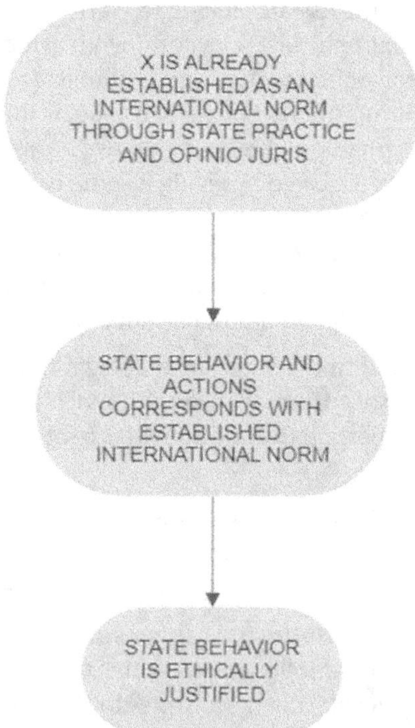

Figure III.2

The disjunctive analysis of *opinio juris* indicates that there does not need to be an assumption that the development of a new custom norm requires the existence of error or deception on the part of a State. This is because the relevant kind of *opinio juris* may correspond with the OJ1 category. Once the customary norm is established, it is sustained by the concept of *opinio juris* as expressed in the OJ2 category above.

The Need for State Consent

The limitations of requiring state consent are easily perceived. The framework for creating consent is an unwieldy, slow process.[1] It creates untold constrictions and invites strategic methods to seek non-consent avenues, which defeats the true purpose of finding common ground for agreement. Even when consent is achieved, it is often reached by weakening the guidelines of a specific agreement.[2] As one expert succinctly puts it, seeking uniformity or general consensus when adopting a convention invites protracted negotiations and ambiguous provisions.[3] Hence, these challenges increase the chance that states will not be party to agreements that resolve difficult issues and are least cost-efficient if an agreement is developed.

The case for requiring state consent involves understanding the seminal role that states play in both the global sphere and in international law. Three assertions make for a consent-based system of international law: (1) To stimulate compliance with international rules; (2) To augment the legitimacy of the international system; and (3) To serve as a protective shield against harmful changes to international rules. Each of these arguments is strong enough to support the notion that state consent is an important requirement in the international system.

Consent and Compliance

One of the strongest mechanisms that the international system lacks is compulsory enforcement. While the Security Council has the authority under the UN Charter to authorize the use of force to maintain peace and security in the global sphere,[4] even these authorizations are predicated on individual states acting. Authorizing or imposing rules on states without their consent may compel the state to simply ignore the rules outright. Requiring state consent ensures the reduction of non-compliance by states by limiting international rules to those states that readily accept them. Requiring unanimity promises, at best, that all affected states prefer the new arrangements over the alternatives. Is there substance to this specific argument? Well, consent may increase the general level of compliance, but it does so at the expense of changing the essence of international law.

An international rule that falls short of achieving perfect compliance may generate compliance pull, which would collaterally or directly change the behavior of some states. With this in mind, a credible international rule with imperfect compliance results could still be a valuable asset and generate the preferred outcome of a particular norm. In short, a defective or inadequate international rule may be more desirable than having no rule at all. For instance, consider Article 8 of the Rome Statute, the prohibition against war crimes. This provision prohibits such conduct as torture, extensive damage to property, and other unlawful crimes.[5] It would be a challenge to find a conflict that did not feature any of the prohibited behavior expressed in the Rome Statute. Despite this instance of non-compliance, such a prohibition is advantageous to the global community and promotes effective reduction of the number of war crimes that are committed.

A state that does not consent to an international norm may be persuaded to comply with the norm if the consequences of non-compliance are unappealing or have disastrous results. When compelled by the global community to adhere to a specific international rule of law, states generally align their behavior with the law in question. Cases that are adjudicated before the World Trade Organization's dispute resolution body exemplify this. When states lose a case before the WTO's dispute resolution body, in a large percentage of these cases, the states comply with the rulings. This suggests that compliance comes about even when states would not have consented to the result, a fact supported by their decision to litigate the issue in the first place.

Consent does not ensure that a state will comply with an international rule. By consenting, states still could violate the law or resist the compliance pull of the norm. For instance, when developing states acquiesced to the Trade Related Aspects of Intellectual Property Rights Agreement, they signed because it was a requirement to join the WTO, not because they wanted to be obligated by TRIPS. Even when a state complies with international law, its position may evolve over time. Iran agreed to the Nuclear Non-Proliferation Treaty in 1968, with North Korea following suit in the 1980s. Iran questioned its signing of the NPT when it explored developing nuclear capabilities,[6] while the North Koreans withdrew from the convention for the same reasons in 2003. While both Iran and North Korea agreed to the NPT, they nonetheless decided to become mavericks and pursue nuclear weapons.

In general, consent represents a flawed alternate for state willingness to comply with international legal rules. Commitments by states often come in the form of reciprocity, where some form of value is exchanged for another form of value. State consent does not guarantee compliance with legal rules. Various multilateral environmental instruments and human rights agreements attest to this fact.[7]

The Legitimacy of Consent

International legal rules created without the consent of affected states encounter problems of legitimacy associated with the practicability of non-consensual rules. In essence, an illegitimate rule may also be deemed an impractical rule. With this in mind, legitimacy could be a good substitute for good rule-making. If a state's willingness to comply is interrelated to the rule's perceived legitimacy, unanimity increases the rule's legitimacy and improves the likelihood that states will comply with the rule.[8] Legitimacy can be ascertained in many ways, but one practical approach is to focus on the process by which the rules are developed. Thomas Franck's *legitimacy theory* and Jutta Brunnée and Stephen Toope's *criteria of legality* support this premise.[9] Legitimacy encourages support for a particular international rule.[10]

There are some ways that harmful rules can be harnessed to improve this process. Thomas Franck's legitimacy indicators can be deployed. These indicators are determinacy, symbolic validation, coherence, and adherence. The first two indicators help ensure that a rule will serve the interests of those who are governed. Determinacy allows the states that are affected to know the meaning of a rule, which gives them the ability to voice their concerns or objections.[11] Symbolic validation involves evidence that a specific authority is being exercised in accordance with the right process.[12] These procedural mechanisms give opponents of proposed international rules the chance to object to a given rule, which heightens the chance that a harmful or bad rule will not be adopted. If dissenting states do not have an opportunity to object or voice their concerns, the global community will have less opportunity to evaluate the rule's merits, which could lead to the implementation of a harmful or bad rule.

In some instances, the concepts of legitimacy and consensus may be inconsistent. This is true within the context of delegated law-making as it is applied within the international system. Delegated law-making does occur within the international system, but it occurs infrequently. The UN Security Council is an obvious international authority that creates binding rules through a voting system. However, the Security Council's authority is qualified. Typical of states is a less vigorous form of delegated authority that facilitates the creation of non-binding legal and quasi-legal rules. The United Nations General Assembly is a prime example of this type of delegation of authority. It is empowered to make resolutions through the process of majority vote, but these resolutions are not binding instruments. General Assembly resolutions can help form customary international law and may even push a legal rule into customary status. There is no consensus on how and when GA resolutions perform this feat, but there is universal acknowledgement that the resolutions of the GA are not (as a stand-alone mechanism) binding international law.

International tribunals represent another form of legitimate non-consensual rule-making. These tribunals generally function under the guise of state consent, but that consent is often provided in advance of a specific dispute. The decisions of these tribunals clarify legal obligations and influence the decision-making process of future tribunals.[13] Some commentators suggest that most states adhere to the rulings of international tribunals because the decisions of tribunals provide an authoritative interpretation of the law and because the possibility of resorting to sanctions as an enforcement mechanism dramatically increases compliance with legal rulings.[14] For example, the decisions of the World Trade Organization's panels and Appellate Body represent a binding declaration on the legality of a disputed trade measure and obligate defendants to comply with the ruling.[15]

Consent is an integral part of delegated rule-making and the dispute resolution process. Parties who partake in the procedural rules expressed in these processes uphold the legitimacy of decisions by granting their consent. This lessens any underlying issues associated with consent because it allows individual rules to develop over the objection of some states. Additionally, some states exploit the gray area that exists between decision-making and consent by creating organizations and practices that are dependent on the delegated consent of states. Upon close examination of state practices, most states have an aversion to giving their consent to the delegated decision-making process. One of the prominent reasons for this reluctance is that the negative results outweigh any positive benefits.

Consent as a Protective Shield

The functionality of consent is more important to the creation of international rules than the connection between compliance and consent. If states are not obligated to consent to international rules that affect them, they would likely lose faith in the rules as a mechanism to protect their interests. Mandating that a state give its consent to a specific rule protects states from international laws that do more harm than good. However, requiring the consent of states is not pansophical nor does it cover all areas. A requirement of consent cannot protect a state from agreements to which that state is not a party. Emblematic of this is the relationship between the Organization of the Petroleum Exporting Countries and non-member states. The members of OPEC have consented to the practices of that organization and enjoy the benefits of that membership. However, some states are harmed by this conglomerate. Because OPEC functions without the consent of those who are harmed by its activities, these countries are not protected by the consent requirement.

Consensus among states indicates that states believe that a proposed rule should be in their best interest. If domestic governments do not represent the interests of their citizens, a state's consent does not guarantee that a specific rule of international law is good for the population of the country. This is one of the chief problems associated with international law. Unless there's an in-depth analysis of a particular state's government, the international system has no choice but to accept the authority of domestic governments to represent the interests of their citizens. A key assumption of rational analysis of states, within the context of international relations, is that states are logical actors that are interested in maximizing the interests of their citizens.[16] Consent, then, becomes a protective shield for both the states and the international system when changes occur that impact the welfare of the state.

The Theoretical Framework of State Consent

Theories that stress the need for state consent in the international legal process fall under the classification of consensualist or voluntarist. These theories address the problem of state obligation in international law, specifically how international legal rules bind states. Underlying these theories are the propositions: "Does state consent, as an isolated concept, propagate customary international legal rules? Is state consent required when it comes to the formation of a customary rule?"

Analysis of Consensualist Theories

From a historical perspective, the requirement for state consent in the legal process originated during the classical period of international law. Classical scholars used the concept of state consent to clarify the development of positive legal rules in a society that did not have a centralized legislative authority. Hence, Vattel and Wolff characterized customary law as the *Voluntary Law of Nations* and asserted that customary rules developed from state consent.[17] The consensualist perspective that has developed since the classical period suggests that: (1) States are sovereign and independent entities; and (2) there is no dominant legislative authority that overrides a state's sovereign rights. They further assert that states make their own laws and they exercise their law-making capacity of their own free will.

The Autolimitation Theory

The autolimitation theory is predicated on the principle that the will of states not only explains why states could be bound by legal rules but also explains the development of legal rules. In essence, international laws are created by and through the will of states, which limits states' behavior when international rules are applied. With this in mind, it is easy to see how the autolimitation doctrine explains the limits placed on states within the international system. However, does this really represent a true limitation on states' autonomy when the operation and function of the international system is dependent upon the will of the state? Thus, if this limitation is based on a state's own will, then states could hypothetically withdraw their consent at will. With this in mind, any binding prescriptive norm or legal rule could not develop out of the autolimitation doctrine: The only thing that could evolve from this doctrine is a political commitment.[1] Considering this, the will of states alone may not qualify as a law-making mechanism. It must also be considered that once a state has given its consent to a legal rule, it cannot revoke it at will. As expressed by the autolimitation doctrine, the irrevocability of a state's will after it has been given could only be valid if a state has first consented to a rule.

If the hypothesis (that a rule is not a legal rule unless its application reflects the will of states) is correct, then it could be argued that consent alone could not possibly create a customary rule because the independent will of the state must be secured before the rule could be applicable.[2] It would be frivolous to draw a distinction between the actual functioning of a legal rule and its development in order to emphasize what role consent plays in the formative stages of a legal rule.

Analyzing the autolimitation doctrine highlights a more fundamental discussion. The doctrine could be interpreted to show that states' rights originate from the concept of sovereignty and that these rights are both extensive and unabridged except in cases where states consent to limit themselves. Regarding this, international law would be little more than a legal system built upon state consent and designed to restrict states' actions and autonomy. In essence, states would be bound solely by a set of norms that explicitly prohibit certain types of conduct, yet free to act as they wish in areas where the law is silent. Disregarding the questions associated with revocability as it relates to voluntary restriction, this view is untenable because, in a community of states, a state's rights cannot be unlimited. In a world where nuclear weapons pose an imminent danger, this would be implausible.

It could be implied that states are keenly aware of this, and it is the chief reason that they voluntarily limit themselves. However, is this limitation based upon their free will, or is it forced upon them by the need to ensure order and security within the global sphere? If the latter were the case, it seems contradictory to uphold a state's sovereignty while simultaneously compelling states to restrict their sovereignty. It would be more practical to assert that states' sovereign rights are *a priori* limited by the fact that other states are also a part of the international system. Even if liberty can only be restricted for the sake of liberty, this justification correlates to the fact that unlimited liberty in any social order is impossible.[3]

In the work *Leviathan*, Thomas Hobbes addressed the issue of unlimited rights and how they impact the law. He noted that while every man has a right to everything,[4] these rights cannot be unlimited at the expense of man's overall security.[5] Hobbes posits two fundamental laws of nature: (1) peace should be the primary objective of every man; and (2) a man should be willing to defend himself when his liberty and security are threatened.[6] Thus, the co-existence of unlimited rights and the law was not practical. His remedy for the problem? There must be a sense of reciprocity: a willingness to limit oneself to the extent to which others do the same. Yet, Hobbes qualifies this willingness within the context of the law of nature. In essence, Hobbes' argument centers on the manifestation of state will as the creator of the law because the law itself is determined by the law of nature.[7]

Commentators such as Lauterpacht and Fitzmaurice dismiss the notion that state rights are originally unlimited. In the case of Fitzmaurice, this notion is both obsolete and unscientific.[8] Both scholars assert that sovereignty in international law is a quality granted by international law through rules that prescribe which given procedures will be observed. However, this argument is problematic. The first issue with this perspective is that it does not account for the origin of secondary legal rules, and the consensualist could easily assert that it represents the consent of states. This perspective also views international law in its entirety, essentially presenting international law as a set of basic laws and principles from which all existing or possible rights are deduced or deducible, and that state behavior and interstate relations are guided and embodied in the corpus of international law. While this proposition could readily be applied during the adjudication process or arbitral procedures, some commentators have expressed the need to acknowledge gaps or gray areas in the law, and creating corresponding rules to address these shortcomings is very important in the international legal system.[9]

If the international legal system is predicated on the concept of autonomy, then its fundamental rules and principles are not easily changed by state will. Proponents of this school of thought could cite Article 53 of the Vienna Convention on the Law of Treaties as evidence that there are rules that cannot be compromised. However, this same article explicitly allows for derogation of those rules by another rule of the same type. Additionally, the fact that these are *jus cogens* rules says nothing about their origins, and a state's consent could have played a seminal role in their formation.

Scholars have long considered the doctrine of unlimited rights for states as an inherently false proposition because a legal right requires the validity of an objective legal system.[10] The concept of unlimited rights is, of itself, irrational. Legal rights are only valid in an environment where autonomy is restricted in some manner.[11] This supports the notion asserted by H.L.A. Hart when he noted that the extent of a state's sovereignty is relative to the rules of the international legal system.[12]

The Theory of Collective Will

Another consensualist theory that needs examination is the theory of collective will. This theory relies on the State will as the source of all legal obligations. There's emphasis placed on the law-creating role of collective will, evolving from the collective will of individual States that have similar objectives. As an isolated framework, this view is unable to explain the law-creating mechanism of collective will. In essence, if the collective will of States formulates laws, then it must have this effect because an international rule requires it. When applied to the customary process, this theoretical framework is problematic.

There is no clear explanation as to whether State will is adequate, even if such factors as uniformity of practice and other external criteria are taken into consideration. However, it could easily be addressed by demonstrating that the State's will is proven by such external factors as uniformity of practice. Even with this proposition, the notion that collective will is an important factor that creates customary international rules seems to be contrary to the distinctive feature that outlines the customary process: the normative role played by State practice.

Jean-Jacques Rousseau developed a theoretical framework—the contract theory—that put forth an entirely different proposition. He asserts that states, like individuals, have an incentive to enter into a contractual obligation when there is no general rule for judging the claims made by one against another.[1] Rousseau attempts to not only justify the basis of legitimate authority within domestic societies, but also put forth a proposition that an act of association involving every individual person creates a moral and collective body that produces a general will.[2] Within this framework, each individual still retains their private will.[3] While Rousseau's hypothesis tries to explain the interrelationship between a sovereign State and a proper will as it pertains to each individual's rights and liberty, it seems somewhat inadequate to apply the same reasoning within the international system because of the simple reason that there is not a sovereign power within the international sphere that has legislative powers similar to a domestic government.

If Rousseau's theoretical framework holds true and the collective will theory follows this analogy, each State is considered an individual and autonomous entity and as a member of a sovereign with legislative authority to enact laws. However, an argument against this assertion could be that legislation is only supposed to be enacted towards third parties and not only towards those who are part of the law-making process. The problem that may arise out of this proposition is whether a State's will, which has already been manifested and integrated into the collective will, can be withdrawn. If this were possible, it's conceivable that individual States that changed their minds would contradict this theory by suggesting that their will is contrary to the will that had previously manifested and still be a part of the collective will. Of course, this is an impossibility.

After close examination, the collective will theory needs to be adjusted or redefined in order to explain the existence of special customs, opposing customs, and individual practices that are different from more established customs. The reason for this? There must, on some level, be an acceptance of the fact that there are differences among sovereign States that entail different approaches to different situations.

State Consent and the Legitimate Authority of Customary International Law

Norms of customary international law present difficulties for international courts. Principles and rules of CIL are unwritten sources of international law consisting of a general practice performed out of a sense of legal obligation (*opinio juris*).[4] *Jus cogens* norms are an integral part of CIL, and eclipse treaty law and other CIL.[5] Scholars and judges may have a difference of opinion about whether an alleged CIL is a rule of CIL, whether it satisfies the two required conditions, its specific contents, and if it is a *jus cogens* norm.

CIL seemingly challenges the role that State consent plays when it comes to accounting for the legitimacy of public international law. Take, for example, the immunity of foreign heads of state, the principle of non-refoulement, or *jus cogens* norms that criminalize slavery, torture, genocide, aggression, and other violations of human rights. Sovereign States are obliged to comply with these CIL norms, even if they have not explicitly consented to them. The question is: How do international tribunals navigate the challenges posed by non-consent-based CIL and State sovereignty? There is the argument that the concept of State consent can be weakened to accommodate various tacit forms that are inherently a part of CIL.

Related challenges can occur when resorting to purely hypothetical consent. Some commentators suggest that in some instances, States have a good reason to be obligated under CIL norms without their consent, in response to specific problems associated with collective and collaborative actions.[6] Such reasoning may illustrate why States comply with certain CIL norms, but it does not explain nor justify why States are bound by such norms. Other scholars argue that consistency is interrelated with consent-based treaty obligations because treaties themselves have an element of custom.

These types of arguments raise other important questions to consider. What role does State consent play? And what to make of the various constraints when consents bind States (as in the case with Articles 48-53 of the Vienna Convention on the Law of Treaties)? Yet, some commentators deemphasize CIL as a source of international law because treaties replace and strengthen such unwritten rules.[7] However, such assertions fail to address other aspects of CIL, such as the authority of the concept of *pacta sunt servanda* as it applies to States' consent.

There are other answers to why and when non-consent-based CIL enjoys legitimacy over States. One proposition is that while States have an obligation to honor treaties, their consent to the treaty also contributes to the States' duty to honor CIL norms. One of the chief normative bases for this type of obligation is the Principle of Non-manipulation. Under this principle, a norm not to violate intentionally creates a duty of expectation.[8]

The objective of these arguments centers on identifying the principle of non-manipulation. These arguments do not lessen the need to justify the *jus cogens* status of some CIL and their constraints on treaties. Nor do they deny that State consent is an important mechanism when States are committing to new obligations. What these arguments suggest is that there are overlapping reasons to approve or support the consent mechanism when it comes to States creating legal obligations.

Challenges and Perplexities Concerning State Consent

There are specific perplexities concerning the relationship between CIL and State consent. Some scholars suggest that it is beneficial to require State consent as the overriding factor of legitimizing the authority of international law. Nevertheless, such a requirement involves some costs: consent by all States serves to prevent agreement on what is the overall good of the global community, which in turn sacrifices the need to address what is important to mankind.[9]

The challenges to State consent as a necessary basis for CIL seem to fail. Take into consideration the argument that State representatives have a presumptive ability to speak and act on behalf of their nation and citizens.[10] State consent based on this premise is obligatory because it supports the notion of moral autonomy on the part of a nation's citizenry. Such a democratic, citizen-oriented assertion appears to conflict with public international law because it is unable to show how authoritarian non-democratic nations can be bound (if they can be bound at all). These non-democracies' claim of acting on behalf of their citizens is *prima facie* false because there is no accountability mechanism that links their decision-making process to the preferences of the citizens.[11]

While there are some arguments that non-democratic States cannot bind themselves by consent to treaties, non-democratic States are nonetheless morally obligated to secure the objectives that are critical to confronting and stopping climate change, human rights violations, and piracy.

The concept of chronological paradox represents another challenge to the argument that State consent is the single reason that public international law obligates States as a legitimate authority. This paradox entails the risk of unlimited regression.[12] In essence, why does State consent bind States? We can look at the reason that States agreed to the legal norm *pacta sunt servanda* in the VCLT to answer this question, but this would be inadequate for the simple reason that various States have not consented to the VCLT. Additionally, how could a State's consent to the VCLT create an obligation if the State's consent had no consequence for the State prior to the State consenting to the treaty? The binding force of State consent cannot act as a stand-alone mechanism.[13]

Some commentators suggest that in order to reconcile CIL with State consent, there must be some type of tacit or presumed consent.[14] However, such assertions are open to criticism and raise questions. As Locke succinctly asks, who has the authority to ascertain the specific content of norms that a State tacitly consents to?[15] Are these norms distinct among a limited group of States, or general in nature? Is there a distinction between normatively binding tacit consent and tacit acquiescence?[16]

The International Law Commission's Conclusions reject the concept of State consent as a credible source for CIL. They note that the abnormal nature of CIL is not based on formal consent. The conclusions include the term *'opinio juris'* next to *'accepted as law'* because it clarifies the nature of the subjective element of customary international law as referring to legal convictions, not to formal consent.[17]

Some scholars assert that these structural challenges and unique features of State consent give reasons to question the importance of consent for issues associated with legitimate authority.[18] We should not indiscriminately disregard State consent because of these concerns. The legitimacy of CIL can benefit from reflections on the reasons that may lead us to believe that consent (generally) and State consent (particularly) grants public international law a certain amount of legitimate authority, which compels States to comply out of a sense of moral obligation.[19]

Complications of State Consent

There are several noticeable roles associated with State consent. According to international standards, State consent must be based on sound reasoning and voluntary to create a legal obligation, not secured through threats or the use of force.[1] Nevertheless, aggressor States may be obligated under the terms of peace treaties even if they sign due to threats carried out in accordance with the United Nations Charter.[2]

States are also bound by some legal obligations without their express consent, such as under *jus cogens* norms, which are accepted and recognized by the international community.[3] In actuality, the number of non-consent-based CIL suggests that State consent is the exception rather than the norm. Consider the deterioration of the persistent-objector rule, third-party effects of treaties giving rise to general practice, majority voting within treaty bodies, the law-making process of international organizations and international courts, and the reservations doctrine emblematic of various treaties.[4] In some cases, States consent to treaties that crystallize existing custom, such as the concepts of *pacta sunt servanda* as expressed in Article 26 of the Vienna Convention on the Law of Treaties.[5] The consent of these States does not create new obligations, but simply recognizes and confirms their consent to be bound. Some customary international laws, such as *jus cogens*, restrict the material contents of the legal obligations States can create through their consent.[6] This can also be achieved retroactively.[7]

Thus, consent plays a seminal role when customary international law compels States to obey and defer to its guidelines.[8] However, consent is neither essential nor sufficient for States to develop or avoid international legal obligations. State consent seems to create new binding obligations within a specific sphere or when certain criterion is met.

The Merits of State Consent

The conditions, limitations, and imperfections of State consent as a necessity for some States' legal obligations help identify the justification for some restrictions on State consent and why customary international law can correctly be considered a legitimate authority. The criteria that define the legitimate authority for States differ from the standards of judges who interpret international law.

Speculating on how well State consent acquires certain values helps appraise both criticisms and improvements to the role of State consent within the international system. On the one hand, State consent may disproportionately give too much prerogative to the *status quo* or give State actors unfettered discretionary power to avoid a morally required obligation or to block agreements that are beneficial.[9] On the other hand, improvements probably would show the value of international law and highlight the mechanism that could fine-tune the conditions and exceptions for when State consent creates binding legal obligations. These improvements presumably also include a better understanding of why and when we have a good reason to value the consent of non-democratic States.

Focusing on the value of State consent may also help to recognize and acknowledge specific non-consent sources of customary international law—whether that source is soft law, the lawmaking authority of international organizations and international tribunals. The lack of State consent associated with the lawmaking authority of international organizations and international tribunals may entail benefits, but it also entails risks—risks that encompass such questions as: Why might a free, sovereign State consent to live under restrictions? What reasons do States have to consent to treaties in order to publicly acknowledge or acquire an obligation to defer to a specific norm and subject themselves to its authority?[10]

State Consent as a Barrier Against Domination

State consent protects States against the risks that other States may arbitrarily impose their will on them. Since each State is sovereign, no other actors randomly determine the options that are the sole domain of other States. State consent implicitly gives a State better control over policies that are in the best interest of the State. If other States acknowledge a State using consent in this manner or essentially attempting to self-bind, the State may obtain results that are otherwise unachievable. The consent must be a catalyst for some new exclusionary or isolated reasons for the State to act otherwise and in a manner that earns the respect of other States. This includes when the State is able to identify and make an informed decision among its various options, and when these preferences are not unacceptable or objectionable to other States. Conversely, State consent is devoid of value when a State is not fully informed of the consequences of its alternatives, acts under duress or is unable to reconcile its preferences with the global community.[11]

The Predictability of State Consent

A State's explicit consent facilitates its future compliance with international norms and helps other States to predict its actions. This procedure is dependent upon a mutual understanding that consent implicitly imposes legal obligations that must be upheld unless some overarching reasons limit a State's action. The value of this process lies in the fact that the State's future actions must be of value to other States. This applies to both non-democratic actors as well as authoritarian actors. The predictability process is applicable to agreements with reservation clauses that call for exemptions, as long as these clauses are not frequently abused. This process only really works when a State or actor acknowledges its intent to uphold a rule.[12]

State Consent and Status Equality

Another important element of State consent is the concept of status equality among States.[13] Thus, if a State enjoys legal sovereignty within a particular domain, it is of value for other States to enjoy the same equality within their particular domain. However, there must be consideration for smaller, non-industrialized States. These smaller States may be at risk of being dominated by larger, more powerful States due to their relative inferiority. One influential commentator expressed it like this: "in entering the Family of Nations a State comes as an equal to equals; it demands a certain consideration to be paid *to its dignity*, the retention of its independence, of its territorial and its personal supremacy."[14] Furthermore, this value does not require a specific issue for the State consent to be binding as long as all States enjoy the same legal domain. One important type of case where State consent may facilitate the values listed above is when consent helps secure cooperative efforts within the international community. The requirement of State consent allows States to maintain global equilibrium based on mutual objectives.

Thus, the requirement of State consent helps promote a more balanced bargaining process while reducing exploitation and domination.[15] However, promoting unanimity may cause States that want a larger share of the benefits to create gridlock in order to obtain their objectives. There are also correlative issues to be considered. States may agree on comprehensive objectives that are proposed but disagree about how to specify them or the requisite strategies to achieve them. Certainly, States do face such multifaceted challenges. Before States can cooperate to enforce an agreement, they must bargain to decide which one to implement.[16] Thus, a State's interest in controlling the final result may serve as an obstacle to achieving objectives for the good of the global community.[17]

Taken in totality, the points above serve as a reminder of the implications when considering the legitimate authority of customary international law. The values of State consent are predicated on some broader account concerning specific domains and the conditions under which State consent is a decisive factor when creating expectations. A State's uncoerced choice among specific options within some domains helps States secure some of their objectives within the global community.

Chapter IV
State Practice

State practice consists of an act, a series of acts, a course of action, or specific behavior displayed by a particular State. On the most basic level, this definition may be satisfactory, but it still leaves unanswered questions that sometimes fall within a gray area. These questions include (but are not limited to) what types of behavior comprise State practice, and which organs of the State are empowered to represent State interests and to act on the part of the State.

An Overview of National Digests and the Concept of State Practice

In determining what is or can be considered State practice, a good blueprint can be found within the annals of official documents developed by States that express their specific practice. Additionally, there are other official publications concerning State practice that receive oversight and guidance by governments, such as diplomatic correspondence. Below is a survey of digests and yearbooks that pertain to the concept of State practice.[1]

The Council of European Resolutions

In examining measures to facilitate the publication of digests of State practice in international law, the Committee of Ministers developed Resolutions (64) 10 and (68) 17, which express their belief on exactly what comprises State practice. Concerning which organ or entity whose practice should represent State practice, the Council indicated that all organs are included. This includes the Executive, Legislative, and Judicial entities and the powers emanating from these bodies.

In identifying official documents that represent State practice, the Council acknowledged two distinct levels:

1. First, it referred to diplomatic notes, letters of instructions, reports, opinions of legal experts, internal memoranda, explanatory memoranda, legal texts and regulations, parliamentary reports and discussions, and the decisions of national tribunals.
2. Second, it acknowledged treaties and conventions to which States are party, statements made before international organizations, statements presented before international judicial or arbitral authorities (only if they contribute to the creation of public international law), and the practice of the State in its relations with international organizations.[2]

Repertoire de la pratique française enmatière de droit international public[3]

This directory of French practice comprises two parts: Governmental and Parliamentary documents, and decisions of the judiciary. Documents from the government and Parliament include:

1. Texts of laws and regulations and explanatory memoranda
2. Reports of Parliamentary committees
3. Reports given to Parliament by governmental officials
4. Replies from government officials to questions presented by Parliament
5. Letters of instructions
6. Diplomatic notes
7. Statements made at international conferences and/or international organizations
8. Opinions expressed by official legal advisors
9. Statements presented before international judicial or arbitral authorities
10. Conventions to which France is a party
11. Press and media communications[4]

Repertório of the Brazilian Practice of Public International Law[5]

This digest includes, inter alia:

1. Statements made at international conferences or international organizations
2. Press and media communications
3. Joint communications between States
4. Diplomatic notes
5. Official reports by governmental representatives to parliamentary committees
6. Debate proceedings in Parliament
7. Internal reports and/or memoranda
8. Letters of instructions
9. Opinions given by official legal advisors[6]

Swiss Directory of Public International Law[7]

This directory includes, inter alia:

1. Diplomatic notes or aides-memoire

2. Statements at international conferences or international organizations
3. Reports or statements by government officials to Parliament
4. Decisions of the Federal Council
5. Governmental circulars to local governments (cantons)
6. Internal memoranda
7. Opinions given by official legal advisors
8. Decisions by the judicial system[8]

Italian Practice of International Law[9]

The Italian Yearbook pertains to documents relating to:

1. The conclusion of agreements (i.e., letters of ratification, full powers, etc.)
2. Letters of instructions
3. Diplomatic correspondence
4. Statements made by government officials to Parliament
5. Parliamentary debates
6. Internal memoranda (governmental instructions and orders)
7. Legislative acts
8. Opinions given by legal advisors[10]

The Digest of United States Practice of International Law[11]

The preface of the Digest explicitly notes that 'practice' is treated as liberally as possible. The materials that pertain to State practice are as follows:

1. Treaties
2. Executive agreements
3. Legislation
4. Federal regulations
5. Federal court decisions
6. Testimony and statements given before Congressional and international bodies
7. Diplomatic notes
8. Correspondence
9. Press conference statements
10. Internal memoranda[12]

The Australian Yearbook of International Law[13]

This Yearbook includes, inter alia:

1. Reports of Parliamentary committees
2. Judicial decisions of national courts
3. Statements and/or replies made by governmental officials to members of Parliament or Parliamentary committees
4. Media and press communiqués or articles generated for publishing by the Foreign Office
5. Statements by representatives at international organizations
6. Legislative acts and explanatory memoranda
7. Opinions given by official legal advisors[14]

The Japanese Annual of International Law[15]

The Japanese Annual of International Law emphasizes:

1. Statements by Government officials to Parliament or its committees
2. Statements at international conferences or international organizations
3. Media and press communications[16]

The Canadian Yearbook of International Law[17]

Canada's concept of State practice falls under three sub-categories:

1. From the Department of External Relations, the materials highlighted include:
    1. Internal memoranda
    2. Opinions given by official legal advisors
    3. Diplomatic notes and letters
2. From Parliament, the following materials are relevant:
    1. Parliamentary resolutions
    2. Statements given to Parliament by Government officials
3. Agreements to which Canada is a party[18]

Documents on Swedish Foreign Policy[19]

These documents on State practice pertain to:

1. Conventions

2. Statements made at international organizations or conferences
3. Replies made by government officials when responding to questions asked by Parliament
4. Media and press communications[20]

The South Africa Yearbook of International Law[21]

When it comes to this Yearbook, State practice is confined to:

1. Statements made in Parliament
2. Statements made by Government officials to Parliament[22]

The British Digest of International Law[23]

The preface sets the tone for the materials that pertain to State practice. State practice encompasses:

1. Diplomatic notes
2. Internal memoranda and reports
3. Letters of instructions
4. Opinions given by official legal advisors
5. Adjudicative decisions given by national courts
6. Texts of laws and regulations
7. Parliamentary debates
8. Statements given by Government officials to Parliament or Parliamentary committees
9. Conventions
10. Statements at international conferences
11. Statements presented to judicial or arbitral authorities and extracts from the decisions of these authorities[24]

An Examination of Case Law

In addition to the previously discussed digests, case law is relevant, particularly when the burden of proof regarding the existence of a customary norm makes it necessary for competing States to present pertinent evidence that supports their notion of State practice. In all these cases, there is no clear indication that the Court dismissed any evidence specified on the ground that it was inadmissible as evidence of State practice. On the contrary, the Court examined the evidence and mentioned some of it in support of its conclusion regarding the existence of a given customary rule. The cases below provide excellent examples of case law as evidence of State practice.[1]

Notable International Law Cases

The *Asylum Case*

In the *Asylum Case*, the Colombian Government attempted to prove its right to diplomatic asylum—including the right of unilateral qualification and the right to safe conduct—based on customary international law. Colombia did this by referring to multilateral and bilateral treaties, diplomatic correspondence, media and press communications, and a memorandum of the Diplomatic Corps.[2]

Right of Passage Case

In the *Right of Passage* case, Portugal presented evidence of treaties, diplomatic correspondence, and correspondence between entities of the Portuguese Government in order to prove the existence of a general and local customary right of passage through enclaves.[3]

US Nationals in Morocco

In the case of *US Nationals in Morocco*[4], the United States used a variety of evidence to establish State practice. This included diplomatic correspondence, treaties and Joint Declarations, the practice of American consular courts, and the decisions of the French judicial system.[5]

The North Sea Continental Shelf Cases

The North Sea Continental Shelf[6] cases offer more details when it comes to establishing evidence of State practice. In this case, three contending States referenced the concept of State practice:

1. The Common Rejoinder offered by Denmark and the Netherlands referenced:
    1. Boundary treaties and other agreements
    2. A Presidential proclamation
    3. An international arbitral decision
    4. Voting positions taken by States at the Geneva Conference on the Law of the Sea
    5. An aide-memoire
    6. Legislative acts and explanatory memoranda

    7. Diplomatic correspondence
    8. A press communication
    9. Presidential decrees
    10. A statement by a Government official in Parliament[7]
2. The Federal Republic of Germany cited:
    1. Legislative acts
    2. Presidential decrees
    3. Various boundary agreements
    4. A Protocol to another boundary Treaty[8]

Nuclear Tests Case

In the *Nuclear Tests*[9] case, Australia and New Zealand attempted to prove the development and existence of a rule of customary international law that prohibited ongoing atmospheric nuclear tests by citing:

1. Multilateral treaties
2. UN General Assembly resolutions and resolutions of regional bodies
3. A Declaration of the 1972 UN Conference on the Human Environment
4. Statements by State representatives before UN entities and at the Geneva Conference on the Law of the Sea
5. A resolution adopted by the Geneva Conference on the Law of the Sea
6. Joint Declarations by Foreign Ministers and Heads of State
7. Diplomatic and public protests
8. A Report to the International Law Commission (by a member of the Commission) on the Law of Treaties[10]

State Entities and the International Legal System

Primarily, States generally value each other within the global community, and acts by States facilitate unity within this community. But the international system is complex, composed of powers and entities that are regulated by domestic legal systems. The entities of a State are generally defined by the power of the internal legal system.[11] The actions and behavior of these entities (or agents of these entities) can result in legal consequences at the international level that either collaterally or directly affect the development of new rules or alter the makeup of old ones. Thus, it is primarily these domestic entities and agents through which the State participates in and ultimately impacts the customary process.

From the rigorous consensualist perspective, there is another qualification applied to the customary process. From the consensualist viewpoint, the entities of the State that take part in the customary process could bind the State to treaties according to the States' own internal laws.[12] In essence, this applies to the States' organs and entities that are responsible for the conduct of foreign relations.[13] However, this hypothesis is problematic because the customary process is essentially a different process from the treaty process, mainly because custom does not represent a (tacit) treaty.[14] Historically, scholars have supported the notion that the potential role of any entity of the State in a given customary process, regardless of its functions, is determined by the internal legal order, whether or not its actions are of an international character.[15]

Evidence of Customary International Law

The examination of the State actions above indicates that State practice pertaining to the customary process could consist of the practice of State entities that come from the executive, legislative, and judicial branches of the government. This is further supported by the position the International Law and the UN Secretariat expressed in the Memorandum *Ways and Means of Making the Evidence of Customary International Law More Readily Available.*[16] The catalogues of evidence of customary international law presented by the Memorandum consist of:

1. Treaties
2. Judicial decisions of national and international courts
3. National legislation
4. Diplomatic correspondence
5. Opinions of national legal advisors
6. The practice of international organizations[17]

Just because a State entity or organ is engaged in domestic activity as opposed to international activity does not diminish its potential role in the formation of customary international law. However, the act or conduct of the State entity or organ must actually encompass a matter of international concern.[18] Thus, these actions, either in isolation or part of a concerted effort, must involve an international issue.[19] In some instances, the actions of different State organs or entities are either consistent with established State policy or subsequently endorsed by it. A State certifies practices of domestic organs when the Executive agency responsible for international affairs confirms its validity with regard to other States.

Role of Non-State Entities

Although State action and overall behavior are highly important to the legal process, it is worth noting that acts and conduct of private persons, private companies, and public corporations play a seminal role in the customary process, if their actions are within their private capacity. For example, when a State is exploring its natural resources in its exclusive economic zone or exploiting outer space, these courses of action are actually undertaken by its nationals or its public or private corporations acting within their private capacity.

There are other instances where the conduct of non-State entities or organs has been regarded as relevant to the formation of customary international law. In the Namibia case, Judge Ammoun noted that the struggle of peoples has been the overriding factor in the formation of customary rules which recognize the right of peoples to self-determination.[20] He compared it with the *general practice* meaning as expressed in Article 38, 1(b) of the Court's Statute.[21]

It must be noted that although acts of individuals or private entities in a private activity may help establish the factual aspect of custom, their actual relevance to the formation of the resulting customary rule (i.e., the normative effects of such acts) is only produced as a direct or indirect participation of State organs.[22]

State Responsibility and the Customary Process

There needs to be a distinction made between the organs, persons, or entities that have the authority to take on the responsibility of the State as a subject of international law and those that can participate in the customary process as a representative of the State. As the International Law Commission's Draft on State Responsibility notes, an act of State, for the purposes of international responsibility, is a somewhat limited concept. In order to characterize this type of State act, it must be performed by an organ or agent of the State, recognized as such by domestic legal authorities. Additionally, this organ or agent must have acted in this capacity alone.[23]

The Draft acknowledges the possibility that actions of private individuals can be attributed to the State, but they must actually be performing public functions or acts on behalf of the State.[24] Why is this requirement so strict? Because the act of State is to be evaluated within the parameters of the 'objective element' to see if the act in question constitutes a failure by the State to comply with the general principles of international obligation.[25]

Position of State Organs in the Customary Process

The position of an organ within the power structure of the State is not a definitive measure for assessing its relevance within the customary process. The practice of a given State on a given issue entails not only presenting a specific claim or performing certain acts, but also enforcing and applying specific claims. Claims may be performed by organs or officials that have a lower position within a State's power structure. This is particularly true when it comes to State regulation over spaces under its sovereignty or jurisdiction.

In some instances, the practice of a State encompasses a set of acts by different organs of the same State performed by officials of varying ranks. This is the case when it comes to a State's Exclusive Economic Zone. Under the EEZ, the zone itself can be established by means of a Presidential Proclamation or an act of Parliament, and further regulated by a Presidential Decree or an administrative Act. It could then be observed by maritime authorities or enforced through the adjudication process.

The question arises as to whether, in comparison to the treaty process, there is a special function among State organs when it comes to the customary process.[26] In a nutshell: No. The functions and competence given to a State organ by domestic authorities or by international law would not justify the difference between the law-creating function and the law application function of a State's organ. Even if such differences did exist, in practice, the function of the State organ does not always correlate with the legal effects that result from it exercising its function.

For instance, within the domestic legal order, an organ whose function is to apply the law may well, in performing its duty, be creating it at the same time. This happens because the creative process is inherent in the application of the law since it involves the choice of law, the interpretation of applicable laws, and their adaptation to the circumstances of the case at hand.

State Practice and *Opinio Juris*

Another interpretation that could be drawn from the above analysis is that there are various acts and documents that articulate or record a State practice. What is most intriguing is the fact that the digests of State practice do not differentiate between acts which represent, or documents which record, the material practice of the State and those which convey the *opinio juris* of the State or its material practice element.

In essence, a broader concept of State practice has been adopted, which encompasses:

1. Both elements of the customary rule

2. The functional element, which has evidential value and, in some cases, has a constitutive quality
3. Both physical acts or conduct, along with formal and informal acts such as public proclamations

A similar approach has been used by States during the adjudication process. For example, in the *North Sea* cases, the Court stated that "the acts must be such, or be carried out in such a way, as to be evidence of a belief that this practice is rendered obligatory by the existence of a rule of law requiring it."[27] In the *Gulf of Maine* case, the Chamber of the Court highlighted the point that customary international law consists of "...a set of rules whose presence in the *opinio juris* of States can be tested by induction based on analysis of sufficiently extensive and convincing practice..."[28] Thus, the Court looks for both elements of customary law in the same material.

Challenges to Broader Notions of State Practice

Over the intervening years, some commentators have challenged the concept of a broader notion of State practice on the premise that only the physical conduct of States or their actual acts should be regarded as an expression of *material practice* which may influence the customary process.[29] The reason for this is to exclude all acts which represent an insignificant claim or declaration from the notion of material State practice, characterizing them as an expression of *opinio juris.*

This seems to be based on perception, because in reality (as the methodology adopted by the Digests of State practice and the reasoning of the Courts shows), any attempt to clearly isolate the two elements of a custom will be a difficult exercise. The relevant instances of State practice or the documents which contain evidence of State practice are mostly those which simultaneously indicate the *opinio juris* of the same State. In addition to this, even if it were possible to clarify the boundary between both elements, this does not mean that claims and declarations could not represent the material element.

On a historical level, it has been noted that sometimes there is little or no difference between what a State does and what it says, and when any noticeable difference is identifiable, the interrelationship between both may be so close that it may be impossible to make a distinction.[30] For instance, there is no physical action or behavior in a diplomatic protest, or diplomatic waiver from jurisdictional immunity: They usually materialize as a formal declaration. Yet, they are considered acts of States and represent State practice.[31] The relevant act is the recognition itself, and it generally comes in the form of a public declaration rather than the exchange of diplomatic representatives.

Claims and Declarations in State Practice

There are also claims and declarations that augment physical conduct, in the sense that they contribute to its clarification and, to that extent, should be regarded as establishing the material element of custom. A good example is the Exclusive Economic Zone. Under the EEZ, it is known that, contrary to the Continental Shelf concept, it has to be expressly claimed by a State before it can enjoy and assert its sovereign rights.[32] In most cases, the Proclamation, which generally comes in the form of a Declaration, Presidential Decree, or legislative act, becomes more of a guideline for all subsequent State practice.

Some scholars have made a distinction between a claim (which comes in the form of a State act) associated with some specific issue or potential dispute, and a 'mere assertion *in abstracto* of the existence of a legal right or legal rule.'[33] Claims expressed as a State act consist of the material practice of States, while the latter augments the evidence of *opinio juris* and State practice.[34] This premise seems to use the concept of claim to make a determination between the material element of custom and, in cases when State practice is not material and only serves as a basis for evidence. But, how can the material element of custom be defined by referencing a non-material concept such as a claim? Basically, a material element should be defined or expressed based on external criteria.

The above approach emphasizes the influence that conflict resolution has when it comes to the developments associated with the custom process. A claim explicitly raises disputes, generally facilitates support from other States, and may even be adopted by other States. There are other questions raised by the above premise. The above premise entails semantics, where assertions *in abstracto* may correlate with the term 'potential dispute,' causing one to relate 'potential dispute' with a situation that 'has not yet' materialized or 'may eventually' materialize. Some commentators have suggested that a claim that bears a resemblance to an assertion in abstraction could have been expressed with a specific or potential dispute in mind.[35]

Physical Assertion vs. Claims

A different perspective disregards the role that claims have in the customary process when they are not supported by physical assertions. A statement made by Judge Read in the Fisheries case represents this viewpoint. Judge Read contends that "customary international law is the generalization of the practice of States. This cannot be established by citing cases where coastal States have made extensive claims, but have not maintained their claims by the actual assertion of sovereignty over trespassing foreign ships."[36]

The concept of effectiveness was likely the defining factor for this conclusion. Under this concept, the effective protection of a claimed or recognized right could validate and consolidate such a right.[37] The concept itself has been an integral part of international law since the mid-20th century and was a decisive factor in the Court cases of the *Nottebohm* case[38] and in the *Minquiers and Ecrehos* case.[39] The concept of effectiveness has merit because it gives recognition and support to the reality that international relations have upon the customary process.

Judge Read's statement could be considered in light of a situation where the State, which makes a claim, can actually enforce that claim, but fails to do so or gives effect to the claim. However, the legal force of actual claims should not be excessive. The Fisheries case highlights occasions when seizures would be irrelevant. These occasions include:

1. When they are met with immediate protest
2. When the asserting government fails to justify and maintain the seizures on the global level[40]

These occasions indicate that conspicuous actions are to be considered in light of all relevant circumstances pertinent to the case, and acts other than the actual conduct are applicable to the custom process.

This perspective can be problematic because it may deceive others into believing that a claim and the actual conduct of a State are entirely two separate things. Of course, there could be some difference between a given claim and the material act carried out by a State. But a claim is more often associated with a specific act or certain behavior of a State, whether that act or behavior takes place in the past, present, or future. A claim generally corresponds to or is associated with a particular act of a State. When a specific or physical act is performed by a State and that act is expressed or follows the State's claim, the two elements augment each other.

Limitations of Physical Assertion Emphasis

However, Judge Read's perspective does have some shortcomings. During the mid-1970s, eight States claimed sovereign rights over segments of a geostationary orbit which was located in the airspace over their territories. During this time period, these States had no way of enforcing their claims. Later, they changed their position by suggesting that a legal agreement gave them equitable access to these geostationary segments.[41] With this in mind, one may surmise whether the change that occurred in their legal position had anything to do with their failure to enforce their claims or was it due to a lack of support from other nations?

There are occasions where a State asserts its claims by seizing a trespassing foreign ship, but the resolution of the issue is done in a way that each party explicitly reserves its legal position.[42] This raises the query: How could the State which effectively asserted its claim by means of a conspicuous act use this precedent against another State in a future dispute of the same nature?

Judge Read's theoretical framework seems indefensible when it is applied to a number of bilateral agreements on fisheries that were concluded in the seventies. Under these agreements, a State essentially allowed another State access to its fisheries resources off its coast, subject to specific conditions. The State to which the access was granted also recognized the powers of boarding, searching, and seizure of the granting State should any of the vessels violate the tenets of the regime. These agreements explicitly maintained that they do not compromise either party's juridical position when it came to the extent of territorial seas or fisheries jurisdiction under general international law.[43]

It is highly improbable that any such seizure would signify the recognition (by the State having access to the fisheries) of the other State's claim of jurisdiction and sovereignty beyond the territorial limits accepted by it. Another matter to consider is whether the fact that States that are in opposition to the extended coastal jurisdiction of another State had to conclude this type of agreement strengthens the position of one State or does it undermine the rule defended by them. Possibly, the States that granted access to their extended coast could argue (at a later date) that the agreement was a particular (and legally authorized) derogation of a general customary rule and should be considered evidence of the existence of a customary norm.

To make matters even more problematic, there are general customary rules (rules pertinent to exploration and outer space exploration come to mind) that develop only after a few States actually perform them. Similarly, there are two conflicting general rules or principles of customary international law that are declared by two groups of States to regulate deep-sea mining when the actual exploitation has not commenced yet. When considering the above analysis, it could be concluded that good judgment is a necessity when assessing the importance of actual State practice when it comes to the development of customary rules.

In light of the expansive interactions that take place on the international level, the various means for acting, reacting, and implementing and expanding the parameters of customary international law correlate with the general attitude of the State on a given issue, and this attitude should be ascertained from the combination of relevant acts and positions taken by States.

The Scope of International Practice and Types of Custom

At the beginning of the 1950s, the International Law Commission accepted a working paper from Manley Hudson, which gave an in-depth definition of the components of a custom, and one of the chief points elaborated upon centered on the material element. The material element consists of a "concordant practice by a number of States with reference to a type of situation falling within the domain of international relations."[1] When asked to clarify the expression 'number of States,' Hudson asserted that he did not believe that the practice of a single State was enough to establish a customary norm.[2] In essence, Hudson acknowledged the probability that custom can be established when two States engage in reciprocal practices. The Court case *Right of Passage* supports this premise. In this case, the Court noted that "it is difficult to see why the number of States between which a local custom may be established on the basis of long practice must necessarily be larger than two."[3]

The number of States involved in a particular practice may fluctuate, so that on this criterion or specific guideline, it could be easier to identify several types of customs. This includes identifying:

1. Bilateral custom
2. Regional custom
3. General custom (custom that is recognized by a majority of the States)
4. Universal custom (custom recognized by all or nearly all the States)

The *Asylum* case is a good example of this. In this case, the existence of an alleged bilateral or regional custom was the issue. The Court acknowledged this possibility, but ruled that such a custom had not been proven. Four of the judges in this case noted the existence of sectional or regional customs within the American Continent as an integral part of American international law.[4]

In the *US Nationals in Morocco* case, the Court acknowledged (and the Dissenting Opinion emphasized) the existence of some pertinent customary rights developing from the capitulations regime and possessed by a few groups of States.[5] The Court recognized a general rule of customary international law in the *Nottebohm* case. In this case, the Court interpreted a rule by which nationality granted can establish a right to diplomatic protection only if there is a substantial relationship between the individual and the State.[6]

Requirements for Different Types of Custom

Categorizing various types of customs according to the number of States participating in a specific practice may be relevant for determining the main features of the customary process and act as a measure for the operational range of each customary norm. For example, regarding bilateral and regional customs, there must be explicit evidence that each State would be bound by the customary rule. The Court addressed this requirement in the *Asylum* case. The Court asserted that the Colombian government should prove that "the rule invoked by it is in accordance with a constant and uniform usage practiced by the States in question, and that this usage is the expression of right... and a duty..."[7] The Court further stated that the party "which relies on a custom of this kind must prove that this custom is established in such a manner that it has become binding on the other party."[8]

In the *U.S. Nationals in Morocco* case, the Court addressed this requirement a step further. In this case, the Court noted that there had not been "sufficient evidence to reach a conclusion that a right to exercise consular jurisdiction found upon custom or usage has been established in such a manner that it has become binding on Morocco."[9] And in another case, the *Right of Passage* case, the Court mentioned that it saw no reason why "long continued practice accepted by them as regulating their relations should not form the basis of mutual rights and obligations between the two States."[10]

Germany used this reference point in the *North Sea Continental Shelf* cases. In these cases, Germany rejected the assertion that the equidistance method was a standardized rule of regional customary law: "No regional customary law on the basic principles governing the apportionment of the submarine areas of the North Sea... can be established without the concurrence of France and Germany."[11] Additionally, Judge Ammoun asserted that "while a general rule of customary international law does not require the consent of all States... it is not the same with a regional customary rule, having regard to the small number of States to which it is intended to apply and are in a position to consent to it."[12] Some commentators have noted that the *ratione personae* or breadth of a rule derived from a bilateral or regional custom would be limited to those States which actually observe it, which mirrors the nature of a treaty.[13]

General Custom and the Question of Generality

General custom, which is another form of custom, is established by a general practice. It is difficult to ascertain the level or extent of generality required by a general custom. There is agreement concerning what is *not* required by a general custom: it is not necessary for all States to follow a specific practice.[14] However, beyond this mutual understanding, no definitive number of States has been established. Some States may even question such a definition, given the various ways that the customs process develops. For instance, in the *Wimbledon* case, the Court inferred a general customary rule, by which the passage of a belligerent warship through an international canal was not inconsistent with neutrality, from only two cases because there was not much material for the Court to rely on.[15]

Some scholars use the term *majority* as a guideline to ascertain the level of generality. But using this barometer is problematic:

1. Is it a "small majority" or "large majority"?
2. Exactly what represents a "large majority"?
3. What if a *representative majority* becomes the standard barometer?

One way to qualify the concept of majority is found in the Dissenting Opinion of Judge Lachs in the *North Sea Continental Shelf* cases. The opinion expressed by the Judge suggests that this type of custom should, in most cases, involve the practice of the "great majority of the interested States."[16]

Binding Nature and Derogation from General Customary Rules

There is a mutual understanding that a customary rule that develops from a general custom is universally binding on States, except in instances where the State opposed the rule from its inception.[17] This umbrella effect of general customary rules is qualified by the concept of *jus dispositivum* – normal international rules can be altered by subsequent norms of the same status. These rules can only be derogated from by means of an agreement *inter partes.* This correlates with the sentiments of Judge Lachs when he stated in his Dissenting Opinion: "without attempting to enter into, still less pronounce upon any question of *jus cogens,* it is well understood that, in practice, rules of international law can, by agreement, be derogated from in particular cases, or as between particular parties..."[18] Likewise, the International Law Commission stated that "the majority of the general rules of international law do not have the character of *jus cogens,* and States may contract out of them by treaty."[19]

Despite the universal acceptance of the theorem, there are implications worthy of consideration. The notion of derogation from general law raises the question about the legal nature of this law. It is unimaginable that any legal system would permit derogation *inter se* from its general rules. If an individual can derogate or evade general rules at any opportunity, then questions arise about the validity of the rule.

Derogation from general law, in the international system, is only understandable if all States participated in the established rule. Why? Law-makers are entitled to derogate collectively from the law they have collectively created. This may be qualified when there is a provision added that states the rule or law is valid when two or more parties agree to the terms. Besides the provisional addendum, the belief that general customary rules are derogable from by agreements *inter partes* may be considered justified under the doctrine *lex specialis derogat legi generali.* This principle essentially means that more specific rules will prevail over more general rules.

Lex Specialis Derogat Legi Generali

The doctrine of *lex specialis derogat legi generali* is an element of legal reasoning that has origins in Roman law. The purpose of the doctrine involves providing a basis for a choice when it comes to resolving two conflicting rules that apply and regulate the same subject matter. The principle of *lex specialis* prescribes that when two rules regulating the same subject-matter conflict, priority is given to that which is more specific.[1]

The Principle as a General Principle of Law

Within the international legal system, Article 38(1) of the Statute of the International Court of Justice is universally accepted as the seminal source of international law.[2] One of the central sources enumerated by Article 38(1) is the general principles of law recognized by civilized nations. This provision mirrors the one contained in Article 38 of the Statute of the Permanent Court of International Justice.[3]

The PCIJ never explicitly referred to Article 38(1)(c) of its Statute, while the ICJ has rarely referred to Article 38(1)(c).[4] The Court has avoided outlining the parameters of this notion or expressly affirmed that specific principles fall within its domain. In the case *South West Africa (Ethiopia v. South Africa; Liberia v. South Africa)*, the Court rejected the idea that the *actio popularis*, or right resident in any society, can take legal action on behalf of the public.[5]

As a result of the PCIJ and ICJ hesitation in relying on Article 38(1)(c), legal experts have not reached a formal definition of the general principles expressed in Article 38.[6] One scholar suggests that this does not matter because the essential characteristics of the general principles corresponds to unwritten legal norms of wide-ranging character, which are recognized in the domestic legal system of States and are capable of mutating into the international legal system.[7]

There is little doubt that the concept of *lex specialis derogat legi generali* fits the definition of "general principles of law" as it is expressed in Article 38(1)(c) of the ICJ Statute, considering that they are:

1. Norms of a general legal reasoning, which
2. Are recognized as such in the majority of domestic legal systems, and
3. Can mutate and be applied within the international legal system.[8]

In the final analysis, general rules of international law that conflict with more specific rules of international law will be subordinate to the more specific norm.

Practical Issues and Limitations

However, there are some practical issues that must be considered. As mentioned earlier, States may withdraw from or exclude themselves from general customary international rules if:

1. The general customary rule is not a *jus cogens* norm; and
2. The agreement does not affect a third party.

The second condition is supported by the notion that a treaty does not create either obligations or rights for a third State without its consent.[9] Difficulties arise when there is a perception that there are general customary rules which inherently require application to and by all States, when it is impossible to isolate the attitude of some States from the attitude of other States.

Regarding this type of situation or these types of rules, it could be argued that the treaty was simply *res inter alios acta*, because the operation of the treaty in question (even if the parties intended to restrict themselves) would directly and necessarily affect the exercise of the rights of other States under general international rules.

The nature of the treaty's objectives and of the general rule subject to derogation would make impossible any practical co-existence and legal compatibility between the legal agreements established by each of them. For instance, if State *B* and State *C* entered an agreement by which State *B* would test radioactive materials on an island that belongs to State *C*, how could a derogation from this rule be affected without impacting the rights of other States? In essence, deviating from the agreement would not only impact the two States that concluded the agreement but also other States.

Another practical example concerns the parallel operation of a treaty. In this case, the parallel operation of an agreement that intends to derogate from the freedom of the high seas customary doctrine by appropriating some agreed-upon areas of the high seas would be unimaginable. Expressing sovereignty over a particular area correlates to a claim of *erga omnes*. There can be no exercise of sovereignty against one State only.

Other situations may be examined in which the exercise of the right to derogate from general customary rules is subject to limitations. If the principle of *jus cogens* is set aside, the function of a derogatory treaty that does not influence the exercise of the rights of other States under customary international law may still face opposition from other States that place a value on international regulatory rules.

In another instance, a more complicated situation could arise. What if there is a general customary rule on an issue that is also regulated by a multilateral treaty? Suppose that both State *B* and State *C* are parties to this multilateral agreement. Could these two States derogate from the general customary rule by a bilateral treaty without breaching the obligations expressed in the multilateral treaty?

Universal and General Custom

Hypothetically, a universal custom is formed when all States or a majority of States within the international system are involved in it. All States or a majority of States must participate in the custom in order for the custom to have the binding effect of a general norm.[10] There are not that many universal norms and customary rules. For example, the Court seems to suggest this when addressing the rules of diplomatic and consular relations:

> The Vienna Conventions, which codify the law of diplomatic and consular relations, state principles and rules... accepted throughout the world by nations of all creeds, cultures, and political complexions.[11]

Some scholars suggest that the fundamental principles of the UN Charter could be considered a universal customary rule of international law.[12] In the Preamble to the 1986 Vienna Convention on the Law of Treaties between States and Organizations or between International Organizations, the principle of *pacta sunt servanda* is acknowledged as being 'universally recognized.'

Categorizing custom, as is done above, is based on the number of States that are involved in a particular practice. The Court and the International Law Commission have developed a different approach when it comes to general and universal custom. According to the approach put forth by these two international entities, these two categories are not formally distinguished from one another, and their rules consist of a single set of customary rules under the subheading 'general rules of international law' or 'rule of general international law.'[13]

The acceptance of these expressions is supported by previous UN multilateral conventions, which explicitly use the term 'rules of customary international law,' the Preamble to the 1982 UN Convention on the Law of the Sea, which states that "matters not regulated by this Convention continue to be governed by the rules and principles of general international law." Article 53 of the Vienna Convention on the Law of Treaties also adds to this by speaking of 'peremptory norm of general international law.' The Court may have preferred a single terminology because it would be difficult to differentiate between the two categories.

However, the main reason may have been that the Court seems to acknowledge the binding effect or normative importance of both types of custom. Some experts assert that both general customs and universal customs appear to support the same range of legal obligations.[14] This may be the reason why the

ILC would rather determine the specific development of a customary rule through referencing the subject matter rather than its form (i.e., whether it represents a universal rule or general rule).

Normative Enhancement of Customary Rules

The unified concept of general and universal customary rules, as it is expressed by the Court, suggests that in some instances there could be a normative enhancement of some general customary rules, which binds them on all States regardless of the status of dissent or differing practices, just as much as universal rules which have universal acceptance.

Hypothetically, if a category of universal customs is acceptable to States, the upgrading of the normative value and metamorphosis of some customary rules into a type of 'superior norm' should be reflected by the wider participation and support by States. This certainly seems to be the case for those customary norms that are possible candidates for the status of *jus cogens*.[15]

Customary International Law: Formation and Objection

General Uniformity

Harmonious practice is a chief characteristic of the material element of customary international law. The Court has acknowledged this seminal requirement.[1] Perhaps one of the chief reasons that the requirement of concordant practice is the paradigm is that if the majority of State practice on a particular matter displays no uniformity, it would be difficult to ascertain the content of a customary rule or even determine if that rule exists.

Uniformity entails the aggregate of State practices as it pertains to international practice. A given international practice is uniform when it has been affirmed by consistent behavior. It assumes the occurrence or recurrence of the same situation, and whenever the situation arises, States tend to respond to the situation in the same manner. But what level or degree must an international practice be uniform? Some legal experts assert uniformity is a complete concept and can be inferred by the practice showing uniformity, "as in the case of total application of the equidistance line..." which indicates customary international law.[2]

Additionally, the Court acknowledged the uniformity criterion in the *Fisheries* case. In this case, the Court stated "...although the ten-mile rule has been adopted by certain States... other States have adopted a different limit."[3] But, there is a different opinion expressed by the Court in the *Nicaragua* case. The Court affirmed that:

It is not expected that in the practice of States the application of the rules in question should have been perfect, in the sense that States should have refrained, with complete consistency, from the use of force... the Court does not consider that, for a rule to be established as customary, the corresponding practice must be in absolute conformity with the rule... the Court deems it sufficient that the conduct of States should, in general, be consistent with such rules...[4]

In essence, minor inconsistencies will not negate a customary rule. But it is good to keep in mind that the Court was referring to general international law when it set forth the elastic requirement of a general pattern of consistency. However, this raises the question of whether this requirement should be applied to bilateral or regional customs, both of which appear to have stricter requirements.

One important point to understand is whether the guidelines for uniformity should refer to the general aspects of the rule or to all its implications or definitions. Many legal rules are composed of many intricate details. The Exclusive Economic Zone is a prime example. The UN Convention on the Law of the Sea contains provisions relative to the breadth of the zone, exploration, exploitation and conservation of living resources, and inherent rights of landlocked States. When considering these provisions, how many of them are expressed in the customary rule pertaining to the Exclusive Economic Zone? The only provisions that relate to the EEZ are those that are found to be uniform in practice, as present in the customary rule. This feature is one reason why, when applying these guidelines, some legal rules are unclear when it comes to defining them.

A good example of this is the *Fisheries* case. One of the complaints of Norway in this case was that the alleged 10-mile rule was not really a rule of international customary law because the respective practice lacked uniformity. The United Kingdom admitted that inconsistency existed when it came to establishing a precise unit, but also pointed out that there was sufficient evidence that indicated the practice showed the existence of a rule of customary international law restricting the width of territorial bays.[5] In short, the general scope of the rule—the restriction of the territorial bays—could be considered uniform, but its definition (the 10-mile width) was not. The United Kingdom argued that both elements composed the rule; the Court felt bound to prohibit it.[6]

The complex nature of an international customary rule may also include the consequence that one of its alleged elements is disregarded due to a lack of uniformity. For example, the Court, in the *Nicaragua* case, asserted that the principle of non-intervention basically consists of a prohibition of States or groups of States from intervening directly or indirectly in the internal or external affairs of other States.[7] Acknowledged as a rule of customary international law by the Court, this rule mandates that various types of intervention be ascertained. The Court highlights the significance of support for subversive or terrorist armed activities within a sovereign State, the use of coercive measures by another State to facilitate political, economic, or cultural behavior, as well as influencing the development of foreign policy.[8]

On some level, these rules could be considered problematic. One of the central issues involves a lack of uniformity in practice. Consequently, the extent of the rule (when it comes to non-intervention) would be proved, but one of its definitions would be disregarded due to a lack of uniformity of practice within the international sphere. Perhaps a distinction could be made, prior to discovering if the practices are uniform, between the primary content of a custom norm and the possible expressions assigned to it when it comes to definitions and applications. This is feasible when the customary rule at hand only offers general instructions that require further development as circumstances change. A good example of this is the Chamber of the *Gulf of Maine* case. This case addressed delimitation of maritime boundaries, and how customary international law "only provides a few basic legal principles and guidelines to be followed."[9]

Individual Consistency

Unlike uniformity, consistency is an element that refers to the individual practice of each State, not international practice. As a concept, consistency is a fundamental part of uniformity. Why? Because if individual State practices are inconsistent, then international practice will also lack consistency. Conversely, if the practice of individual States is consistent, international practice may still lack uniformity. A consistent practice is defined as a State behaving in a similar manner whenever the same situation occurs. A very good example is the *Asylum* case, in which the inconsistency of State individual practices was considered in order to invalidate the existence of a uniform international practice.[10]

What specific level of consistency is required for a State practice? According to the Court in the *Fisheries* case, there only needs to be a general level of consistency. The Court asserted that too much importance need not be attached to the real or perceived uncertainties which the United Kingdom Government claims to have discovered in Norwegian practice.[11] This may incur problems. If the individual practice of States is required to be only generally consistent, and if international practice is required to be only generally uniform, then the question becomes: To what extent would the customary rule reflect the common features present in each practice? In another instance, a general consistency is justified in order to discredit the value of a conduct which deviates from a regular pattern of behavior by reason of geopolitics.

The *Asylum* case covers this issue with clarity. In this case, Judge Azevedo questioned the reasoning of the Court because he felt that the examples of interruption in the practice were relatively few and occurred after a consistent pattern of past practices. These interruptions could be considered as breaches of a customary rule previously accepted. If Judge Azevedo was correct in his analysis of the practice (that they were essentially minor interruptions to an otherwise settled practice), then the Court likely concluded that general consistency in practice was insufficient. This analysis mirrors the reasoning in the *Fisheries* case. A noteworthy point was made by Judges Forster, Bengzon, Arechaga, Nagendra Singh Ruda in the *Fisheries* case's Joint Separate Opinion. These Judges asserted that this criterion should be more strictly applicable to those States which are said to be following or establishing international customary law.[12]

Continuity and Repetition

The legal notion of customary rules has its antecedents in classical legal history. The classical writers considered 'long usage' as a defining element of international customary law.[13] Undoubtedly, the Court or individual jurists have found in some cases the existence of long-established custom.[14] However, in modern times, the notion that a particular international practice should be established for a specific time period before it is considered custom is no longer the prevailing notion. A new approach to this matter considers the pace of contemporary international relations, coupled with the innovative mechanisms used for developing customary international law.

During its early years, the International Law Commission addressed this matter. It was concluded that continuation or repetition of a particular practice over a considerable time period represents the best definition of a custom rule.[15] The word 'considerable' seemed problematic, and it was replaced with the word 'some.'

The time requirement could be either short-term or long-term, depending on the nature of the issue or the integral details of the legal process. For instance, concerning the legal process, the occurrence of a multilateral codification conference may facilitate the legal process, as Judge Tanaka alluded to in the *North Sea* cases.[16] However, the most important elements to conclusively establish a custom involve the verification of general, uniform and consistent practice, and *opinio juris*. This is mostly due to the extensive nature of international interaction and the growth of international law itself.

If an established practice has been in operation over an extensive time period, the stronger the custom. This, according to Judge Armand-Ugon in the *Right of Passage* case, is the central function of the time element.[17] Judges Hackworth, Badawi, Levi Carneiro, and Rau, in the *US Nationals in Morocco* case, highlight this point. They asserted that France could not dispute the existence of a long-established customary rule when the "usage has been continuously at work... during a period of nearly a hundred years, if not longer" and that "this usage has been a continuous process" long before the 1930s.[18] Likewise, the system of delimitation applied by Norway in the *Fisheries* case had "been consolidated by a constant and sufficiently long practice."[19] While the time element could not be considered the defining element in the development of a custom, it only serves as evidence that a practice has been established. Historically, some commentators suggest that this should not continue to be a part of the corroborative process of custom since custom expands and embraces rules which are not customary in the strictest sense of the word.[20]

The requirement of continuity may be certified when the general practice that is under examination has not suffered major interruptions during the developing stage. If there have been major interruptions, then the evolution of a general rule may have been barred. In this sense, continuity is similar to the requirement of uniformity. Thus, repetition of practice would be an integral part of State practice. But repetition, as it applies to the development of custom, raises some issues. For instance, should it be expected that every State repeatedly perform the same act? This would engender problems because in some situations, States have no need or interest in acting or reacting again over a particular matter. In the *North Sea* cases, Judge Lachs' comments support this proposition. He pointed out that frequency may be invoked "only in situations where there are many and successive opportunities to apply a rule."[21] There is also the issue of deciding which act or acts to apply when considering the repetition criterion.

The Persistent Objector: Historical Background

In the seminal work *Principles of Public International Law*, Ian Brownlie depicted the persistent objector doctrine as a principle that is an inherent fact of international law.[22] However, the doctrine has been a part of international law since the 1700s. The International Law Association noted that Cornelius van Bynkershock's 1721 work helped facilitate acceptance of the persistent objector doctrine.[23] Bynkershock suggests that dissenting States may be exempt from a custom rule by expressing their will to oppose the rule:

Can a nation abolish the immunities of ambassadors, which they are enjoying in accordance with the common law of nations?... [I]t can if it makes a public announcement in regard to them, because these immunities owe such validity as they have not to any law but only to a tacit presumption. One nation does not bind another, and not even a consensus of all nations except one binds that one, isolated though it be, if it is independent and has decreed to use other laws... The law of nations is nothing but a presumption based on custom, nor has this presumption any validity in the face of a definitely expressed wish on the part of him who is concerned.[24]

A prominent scholar of international law researched and found other sources from the eighteenth century that give evidence of the early embodiment of the persistent objector doctrine.[25] This scholar, James A. Green, notes that Emer de Vattel's 1758 monograph is the first source:

When a custom or usage is generally established... between all the civilized nations in the world... it becomes obligatory on all the nations in question, who are considered as having given their consent to it, and are bound to observe it towards each other, as long as they have not expressly declared their resolution of not observing it in the future.[26]

The second source put forth for the historical basis of the persistent objector doctrine comes from Georg Friedrich von Marten's 1788 assertion that:

As to rights found on simple custom, each power may determine them whenever it makes a timely declaration, either express or tacit, of its intention so to do. Such rights may also cease by giving place to others, established by the mutual will of the nations concerned, but this change made by some powers cannot oblige other powers to change their conduct.[27]

Green determined that although the above sources bear a similarity to the persistent objector doctrine we are familiar with today, these sources lack the modern requirements of consistency, persistence, and timeliness.[28] He also stated that it is a stretch of the imagination to identify the persistent objector principle in the writings of Bynkershoek, Vattel, or Martens because these writers did not ascertain the principle as we do in contemporary times.[29] But, legal principles evolve over time and space, and the persistent objector doctrine of the eighteenth century would indeed differ from the doctrine of modern times.

During the nineteenth century, the persistent objector doctrine transformed from being a hypothetical mechanism to a practical instrument. In the 1817 case *Le Louis*, Sir William Scott, Senior Judge in the High Court of Admiralty, considered whether international law compelled France to prohibit the slave trade.[30] Scott reasoned that while other States had abolished the slave trade, the rule was not applicable to France because it had opposed such a prohibition.[31]

In the 1825 case, *The Antelope*, the U.S. Supreme Court seemingly found the application of the persistent objector doctrine.[32] *The Antelope* case required the Court to determine if the seizure of a Spanish slave ship by U.S. privateers was lawful.[33] Justice Marshall asserted that while slave trading runs counter to the law of nature, States had not accepted the law of nations' prohibition on the practice, and thus there was no violation of a law when trading in slaves.[34] In essence, Marshall relied on the lack of acceptance of the rule that prohibited slave trading rather than on the precept of rejection or objection.

In the *Paquete Habana* case of 1900, the U.S. Supreme Court asserted that customary international law is applicable "where there is no treaty, and no controlling executive or legislative act or judicial decision."[35] Some scholars suggest that the Court, in this case, viewed customary international law as binding on the United States only to the extent that the country did not oppose it.[36]

The 1903 *Fischbach and Friedericy* cases provide another example of the early uses of the persistent objector doctrine.[37] The Mixed Claims Commission was established to consider German claims originating from foreign debts and damages incurred during the Venezuelan civil wars of 1898 to 1900.[38] The Commission's primary duty was to ascertain whether international law holds States responsible for the seizure by revolutionary forces. Arbiter Duffield noted that "[a]ny nation has the" authority and "right to dissent from a rule" of international law even if other States accept the rule.[39] However, Duffield qualified his assertion. He reasoned that Venezuela could not exempt itself from the customs rule because it had previously accepted responsibility for the revolutionaries.[40] At the very least, this decision indicates limited support for the persistent objector principle.

The Persistent Objector and Original Consent

Original Consent as a Foundation for Universalism

Universalism is the primary basis for original consent. For instance, the Universal Declaration of Human Rights and the Vienna Declaration recognize that a State's informal consent to human rights norms correlates with the concept of universalism. Because of this, if a State engages in a particular set of human rights rules but decides later not to participate in the rules because of its objections to the rules during the developmental stages, in all likelihood, the State's refusal to participate could be unlawful. Theoretically, this is because the State has already consented to the universality of the rule, and refusal to participate would be equivalent to violating the State's original consent.

While informal consent could not be considered binding, the principal factor to take into consideration is that the universality of the rule that the State informally consented to is the framework that stabilizes the international legal community. Original consent is a vague but practical interpretation because it could be the basis for persuasive evidence by legal experts, and most importantly, there is no real doctrinal requirement for the strict interpretation of consent.

Original Consent Challenging the Persistent Objector Doctrine

The principle of original consent, by its nature, challenges the strict interpretation of the persistent objector doctrine. The central feature of this challenge lies in the fact that recognition of the persistent objector doctrine implicitly means that the principle of consent is not absolute. The first of these facts concerns the exception given to the principle of *jus cogens*. Very few rules attain the status of *jus cogens*, and within the *jus cogens* exception lie two separate and unequal systems:

1. One for the high half of the *jus cogens* system, and
2. Another for the lower half of the *jus cogens* system.

The fact that there are two uneven systems within *jus cogens* suggests the lack of inclusiveness, which is contrary to the concept of universality. Another matter to consider when it comes to the principle of *jus cogens* is that the principle is vague and could be subject to discretionary interpretation.[1] A good example of this is the Inter-American Commission of Human Rights and its discretionary ban on juvenile executions.[2] The Commission's reasoning that banning juvenile death penalties was on an equal level with genocide (a *jus cogens* principle) should be considered erroneous. The Commission would have been more reasonable if it had focused on the original consent of the United States when it came to the universality of human rights, rather than stretching the parameters of the *jus cogens* principle.[3] In short, the Commission could have reasoned that the persistent objector doctrine could not override the principle of original consent.

The Problem of Foreseeability in Customary International Law

The preservation of foreseeability is the next issue that needs to be critically assessed when it comes to the persistent objector doctrine. There is no set time frame in which customary international law ripens, and it is even more difficult to ascertain when these laws become ripe. To address this problem, international tribunals turn to international case law as a subsidiary source of law.[4] Consequently, after a norm has been declared as customary, States should be advised that the customary international law has ripened. This step adds the essential element of foreseeability.

Traditionally, the persistent objector principle has performed this role. A State that objected to a particular norm could use the rule to determine when to stop objecting and when to accept the fact that the norm has ripened.

Essentially, this doctrine reduces the negative effects of unforeseen liability. However, the foreseeability concerns would likely be more stabilized if the international courts used case law as a subsidiary source. Considering the diminishing role played by consent in international law, the argument that the doctrine is fundamentally unqualified when it comes to consent in international law is debatable.

The role of consent relative to the persistent objector doctrine is constrained when considering such things as a State's original consent to the universality of human rights norms. In truth, the doctrine's only effectiveness could be in a limited number of cases where the major issue centers on the ripeness of a particular norm. The motivation for applying the persistent objector doctrine is when ripeness is the overarching issue.

Treaties, Customary International Law, and the Persistent Objector

There must also be an analytical relationship between treaties, customary international law, and the persistent objector doctrine. Customary international law, in some instances, takes precedence over treaty law. When principles in a treaty have ripened into customary status, then those principles take on the position of universality and apply to all States (including those who did not sign the treaty).[5] In some cases, States can use treaty reservations as *prima facie* evidence of their objection to a particular international norm, which exempts them from the rule even after it has ripened. With this scenario in mind, a State that signs a treaty can use the reservation attached to the treaty as an exemption, but not until the particular reservation is ranked lower in the hierarchy of customary international law.[6] But what about the relationship between the persistent objector and *jus cogens* norms? We know that under no circumstances may any *jus cogens* norms be derogated. We are also aware that under special conditions, a State may derogate from customary international law for national security purposes. This is just an example of the duality that surrounds the persistent objector doctrine.

However, the persistent objector is more than a contradictory concept in international law.

The Persistent Objector: Further Analysis

The practice of dissenting States can be viewed from two different perspectives:

1. The general effect that the objection has upon the customary process, and
2. The binding scope of a specific custom in relation to the dissenting State(s).

The first category deals with the objection of a State or some States to a customary practice during the developmental stages of the custom, which prevents it from further development. The second category is somewhat problematic.

Scholars agree with the concept that a State which consistently opposes a custom from its beginning may prevent the customary rule from being applicable to it.[7] There are two seminal Court cases, the *Fisheries* case and the *Asylum* case, that are used for judicial precedents.

The *Fisheries* Case

Regarding the *Fisheries* case, the Court asserted that it did not perceive in the Norwegian practice any opposition or breach to the general rule itself, but rather a specific application of the rule:

> "Consequently, the Court is unable to share the view of the United Kingdom Government, that 'Norway, in the matter of base-lines, now claims recognition of an exceptional system'. As will be shown later, all that the Court can see therein is the application of general international law to a specific case."[8]

While the Court examined whether the Norwegian system of delimitation would be valid supposing that the alleged 10-mile rule was considered a general rule under customary international law, it is uncertain whether the Court reached its conclusions by considering the *ratio*. Regardless, the Court took into consideration Norway's opposition to the rule as an important element. It concluded that the rule would have been inapplicable against Norway because she had "always opposed any attempt to apply it to the Norwegian coast," and also because there was no opposition on the part of other States to this practice, specifically from the United Kingdom.[9] The Court also noted that the Norwegian practice was both lengthy and consistent.[10] All of these elements of the Norwegian practice were considered in their totality to justify the validity of Norway's practice "even if the alleged 10-mile rule had become a general rule of international law."

What the Court found was not only a case of persistent objection but also a special application of a general rule. Certainly, a conclusion could be made about the application of the persistent objector rule, and there could be a strong case made that the persistent objector principle is a part of the corpus of the *Fisheries* case. If the conclusions made apply *mutatis mutandis* to the case of the persistent objector, the following guidelines should be fulfilled by the State that claims this position:

1. A clear, consistent, and sufficiently long opposition to a practice from the beginning, and
2. Acknowledgement by other States that this opposition exists.

The *Asylum* Case

The *Asylum* case is also similar to the *Fisheries* case in this manner. The relevant statement made by the Court is as follows:

> "Even if it could be supposed that such a custom existed between certain Latin-American States only, it could not be invoked as against Peru which, far from having by its attitude adhered to it, has on the contrary, repudiated it by refraining from ratifying the Montevideo Conventions of 1933 and 1939, which were the first to include a rule concerning the qualification of the offence in matters of diplomatic asylum."[11]

This pronouncement by the Court essentially assumed that the Montevideo Convention is a declaration of a pre-existing custom and that Peru would have repudiated such a custom by not ratifying it. If this assumption is right, then there is no justification to apply the persistent objector principle in this case. Why? Because in this case, Peru could not be said to have been in opposition to the custom since its formation. Peru would have rejected an already established custom rule. Additionally, it is questionable that the failure to ratify a declaratory treaty could exclude the State from the binding scope of the customary rule that is being declared. What makes this so questionable is that it does not envision the possibility that Peru failed to ratify the Conventions for reasons other than disagreement with their relevant provisions.

It can be problematic because of one central question: How can you infer from a single act or omission a pattern of persistent objection to a particular rule? The Court's reasoning could only be explained if you accept the fact that the Court supported the consensualist view when adjudicating the case (which suggests that these types of custom, both bilateral or regional, required the consent of each State involved in the issue). With all things considered, the *dictum* of the Court may be regarded as apparently showing that Peru had not positively consented to the alleged custom, which is entirely different from the finding that Peru had actively dissented from the alleged custom. In short, on the basis of the Court's reasoning and the circumstances of the case, one could not deduce that the principle of persistent objection existed.

Even if the Court had depended on the general attitude of Peru towards the alleged rule, and not only on the failure to ratify the Montevideo Conventions, proving the existence of the persistent objection principle would be difficult. The evidence presented throughout the case indicated that there was a body of

Peruvian practice which made it very hard to prove that Peru had been consistently objecting to the alleged rule or even consistently following it. As noted previously, the Court found a glaring absence of uniformity in the instances of practices by Colombia.

Limitations of the Persistent Objector Doctrine

If bilateral and regional customary rules are considered to be uncompromising or unyielding, the persistent objection principle would only be meaningful to general customary rules. Some commentators have opposed this proposition.[12] To assert that a State may use the persistent objector principle to opt out of a developing bilateral or regional custom seems to be theoretical based since the State could prevent the application of a rule by simply not taking part or supporting the emerging norm, regardless of whether other States acquiesce to the rule.

Additionally, if the requirement of consistent objection to a norm during the developmental stage is fulfilled, it would only apply to evolving general customs, not those customs that have been long established. In essence, a State could not claim a special right derived from an alleged persistent objection to an established general customary rule. Otherwise, the concept of voluntarism would return to international relations, a concept which has previously been rejected by theory and practice. Although an objection by a State to an established general customary rule could undermine it to some degree and, if followed by other States, set into motion a new customary process, it would normally be considered a breach of the rule by other States. This additional requirement of the theory would make its successful applicability highly unlikely or, at the minimum, very restricted.

It is important to note that some commentators consider the inherent differences between the *Fisheries* and *Asylum* cases as they pertain to the persistent objector rule. For example, Patrick Dumberry asserts that "the only ICJ decision that ever dealt with the question of persistent objector in the context of 'general' customary law is the *Fisheries* case."[13] He argues that the *Asylum* case was irrelevant since it deals primarily with regional custom.[14] The relevant quotation in the *Fisheries* case, he notes, is "a mere *obiter dictum*; the Court had already decided to reject the existence of any customary rule on other grounds."[15] Holning Lau suggests that "in both cases, the ICJ's recognition of the persistent objector doctrine was purely dictum and the ICJ had resolved the disputes on other grounds."[16]

Case Studies: France and South Africa

There are arguments that France and South Africa are representative of how the persistent objector should apply. The French officials opposed the definition assigned to the *jus cogens* principle in the final draft adopted by the Vienna Convention on the Law of Treaties, and this was the singular reason they refused to sign the Convention.[17] However, the Conference records indicate that France did not oppose the concept of *jus cogens.* The records suggest that France supported the idea of this principle. The French representative stated:

> "The substance of *jus cogens* was what represented the undeniable expression of the universal conscience, the common denominator of what men of all nationalities regarded as sacrosanct, namely, respect for and protection of the rights of the human person."[18]

However, what would have happened if France had consistently objected to the concept of *jus cogens*? Could it have been successful in doing so?

In the case of South Africa, it admitted to some discriminatory practices as the natural evolution of any country, but suggested that there were breaches of 'ideas' expressed in the UN Charter that had been remedied because it did not condone discrimination solely based on race.[19] One could suggest that South Africa did not openly and consistently defy the rules on Apartheid or racial discrimination, even though its application or interpretation of actual practice indicated the opposite. But even if South Africa had been a persistent objector to these rules, the global community would have still condemned its actions. Thus, South Africa could not conceivably make such a claim due to the universality of *jus cogens* norms.

The Role of General Acquiescence

The requirement of general acquiescence when it comes to opposing a practice seems to conform to the reality of interstate relations. This is all the truer when it comes to recognizing rules of general customary laws that are implemented to act as a protected shield for social values that are considered fundamental by the global community. The Court seems to agree with this proposition when it comes to rules outlawing genocide, slavery, racial discrimination, the illicit use of force and intervention, and rules on diplomatic immunity.[20] It is safe to say that if a State ever challenges such a rule on the basis of the persistent objector doctrine, it would encounter strong opposition from other States, which would make it very hard to assert any special right.

Therefore, in the *Fisheries* case, the Counsel for the United Kingdom asserted one of the exceptions to the persistent objector principle, that: "where a fundamental principle is concerned, the international community does not recognize the right of any State to isolate itself from the impact of the principle."[21] As indicated by South Africa's actions, even in those cases where the dissenting practice concerns what had traditionally been accepted as a reserved domain of the State (the treatment of its own citizens), the other States have been prepared to apply pressure on the dissenting State until the general rule is respected. The practice of UN entities in their interpretation of Article 2(7) of the UN Charter, along with relative State practice, has been evidence of the limited role of State sovereignty when it comes to contesting a *jus cogens* norm. Acquiescence by other States seems to be the overriding factor when applying the persistent objector doctrine.

The acceptance by other States seems to apply to other fundamental rules. For instance, the right that a dissenting State claims directly affects the rights of other States when recognizing an accepted rule. When this happens, it is hard to understand how the persistent objector could exercise its claimed right if not by the previous consent of or acquiescence of other States. What if, for example, a State has persistently dissented from any claim of exclusive rights over the continental shelf that extends beyond the 50-mile limit? Although the State could maintain its claims of 50 miles, it could not legally exploit the continental shelf of other countries located beyond the 50-mile limit when the claims of those other countries correlate with a generally accepted rule, unless they agree to allow it one way or another. Something like this actually happened when some States opposed, consistently, the extension of the territorial sea beyond the three-mile limit. Several treaties had to be developed in order to obtain permission from other coastal States for fishing rights off their coast, while the latter could freely exploit the natural resources beyond the three-mile limit.[22]

Implications and Conclusions

Noteworthy, the successful application of the persistent objector doctrine really means that a potential unilateral opposition to a specific rule has been recognized and runs parallel to international customary rules that otherwise conflict. Once the opposition to the rule is allowed, it becomes an exception to the general rule. As acknowledged by one commentator, recognizing a dissenting position simply creates a particular legal agreement between the dissenting State and the States which acknowledge and allow the dissent.[23]

The persistent objector principle has been called an important device that supports and strengthens sovereign equality among States.[24] However, when it comes to the customary process, sovereign equality is a relative concept because some States have a more decisive participation and greater influence than other States. The main reason for this is that what counts in the customary process is State practice, which has a variety of forms and effects, whereas in the treaty process, the formula "one State, one vote" for the conclusion of the agreement formally secures the equal participation of States. This explicitly reflects the sovereign equity principle.

Additionally, once a customary rule is developed, its far-reaching binding effect (encompassing States which never consented to it or dissented from it) is another limitation imposed on the sovereignty of States.[25] Unless there is a change forthcoming to the voluntarist approach, which gives cadence to the concept of absolute sovereignty, the sovereignty equality principle will always contain some type of limitation. Some scholars suggest that the persistent objector principle acknowledges "the special equities of vested or acquired rights and interests."[26] This assertion is shrouded in controversy: a previously legal situation which subsequently becomes illegal by virtue of the development of the legal issue at hand. In many ways, this highlights the problem of chronological law. In the *Island of Palmas* case, Max Huber commented upon the following principle:

> "The same principle which subjects the act creative of a right to the law in force at the time the right arises, demands that the existence of the right, in other words its continued manifestation, should follow the conditions required by the evolution of the law."[27]

Taking this principle into consideration, the right of the dissenter would be predicated on the evolution of general international law. The Court has shown a tendency to support the new development of the law, whether relying on past legal situations.[28] In the final analysis, the persistent objector doctrine assumes that the law is established and the objector State applies the developing law rather than the law of the past.

Chapter V
The Subjective Element

The subjective element (or *opinio juris* as it is commonly known) is probably the most contentious issue in customary international law. The doctrinal debates surrounding the subjective element may be attributed to the various perspectives of writers when confronted with this concept or to the way writers view the developmental process of the customary process. Regardless, it is an essential element when transforming a general rule into a binding rule. While it, in the words of Emily Kadens and Ernest Young, has been a fundamental problem in theorizing customary international law[1], it is worthy of further examination.

Theories Related to an Established Customary Rule

The Court and Case Law

The reasoning of the Court on the subjective element clarifies the issue. On various occasions, the Court has made it clear that the elements of State practice and *opinio juris* are the essential requirements when ascertaining a customary rule.[2] Yet, the Court's acknowledgement of the subjective element cannot be considered uniform nor exhaustive. The significance of the Court's reasoning lies in the many ways and different perspectives it addresses the subjective element. An itemized list shows how the Court addresses the subjective element, with each category identifying and clarifying the analysis of the Court's reasoning.

1. The Subjective Element as a Belief in a Set of Legal Correlatives

The analytical ruling of the Court in the *Right of Passage* case indicates that it looked for evidence of a right and corresponding duty in the practice at hand in order to ascertain whether the practice aligned with a customary rule. In a preliminary and general statement concerning the possibility of a bilateral custom, the Court stated that the custom, once it was accepted by the parties as regulating their actions, constituted *"mutual rights and obligations."*[3] When the Court decided to analyze the practice of private individuals and civil officials, it concluded that it had given emphasis to a right and correlative obligations.[4] In short, the subjective element was expressed by one State as having a right and another having corresponding obligations. The Court considered the legal relationship or legal foundation built on mutuality and correlativity. This means that determining one often meant determining the other. Thus, when the Court reasoned that there was no right of passage in regards to the armed forces, armed police, and arms and ammunition, it essentially excluded the existence of a *correlative obligation.*[5] From this framework, one could theorize that the subjective element is representative of a legal relationship, which is revealed in the form of legal correlatives (legal right-legal obligation).

The *Asylum* case seems to have the same type of reasoning. In this case, the Court asserted that in order for the alleged custom to be considered established, the usage should be the expression of "a right appertaining to the State granting asylum and a duty incumbent on the territorial State."[6] The *US Nationals in Morocco* case represents another instance where the Court applied such reasoning. After using a passage from the *Asylum* case as a reference point, it affirmed that there was not enough evidence to indicate that a "right... has been established in such a manner that it has become binding on Morocco."[7]

2. The Subjective Element as a Belief in Legal Duty/Obligation

The Court, in the *North Sea Continental Shelf* cases, stated that the belief, by the States, that their actions or the manner in which they behave, was "mandatory" or obligatory in nature represents a sense of legal duty.[8] These, and other comments by the Court, make it clear that, in looking for the subjective element, it considers the subjective element akin to an obligation established by customary rule. On the contrary, in the *Right of Passage* case, the Court did not mention a right nor a correlative obligation, only a legal obligation. The Court used this same approach in the *Lotus* case in order to rule against the French arguments concerning the existence of a customary rule. In the Lotus case, the Court referred to a "sense of legal duty."[9]

3. The Subjective Element as a Belief in a Legal Right

The Court, in the Nicaragua case, inquired into the possibility of a customary rule allowing intervention by States in support of an internal opposition in another State. It explored the existence of a "...belief in a kind of general right for States to intervene, directly or indirectly..."[10]

4. The Subjective Element as a Recognition of the Validity of a Rule in Conventional and Customary International Law

In the *Nicaragua* case, the Court seemingly painted the subjective element as a recognition as an integral part of customary international law and the conventional rule of law. One of the most significant passages states: "... apart from the treaty commitments binding the parties to the rules in question, there are various instances of their having expressed recognition of the validity thereof as customary international law in other ways."[11] The Court further stated that:

> "the attitude referred to expresses an *opinio juris* respecting such rule (or set of rules), to be thenceforth treated separately from the provisions, especially those of an institutional kind, to which it is subject on the treaty-law plane of the Charter. A further confirmation of the validity as customary international law of the principle of the prohibition of the use of force expressed in Article 2, paragraph 4, of the Charter of the United Nations may be found..."[12]

5. The Subjective Element as the Opinion on the Content of a Customary Rule

In the *Nicaragua* case, the Court uses the subjective element to imply the view of States when it comes to the content of a customary rule. The passage concerning this states: "...in the field of customary international law, the shared view of the parties as to the content of what they regard as the rule is not enough. The Court must satisfy itself that the existence of the rule in the *opinio juris* of States is confirmed by practice."[13]

6. The Subjective Element as a Factor That Determines Legally Relevant Omissions

The Court, in the *Nicaragua* case, highlighted the point that the failure by the United States to invoke or recognize a right or rule reflected its *opinio juris* regarding the non-existence of such right or rule.[14] The Court asserted:

> "In the discharge of its duty under Article 53 of the Statute, the Court has nevertheless had to consider whether such a right might exist; but in doing so it may take note of the absence of any such claim by the United States as an indication of *opinio juris.*"[15]

In the *Nottebohm* case, the Court regarded some instances of omissions as evidence of *opinio juris* concerning the validity of a customary norm.[16] In the *Lotus* case, the Court considered some instances of omissions not sufficient to demonstrate an alleged custom norm because the subjective element was not proven.[17]

7. The Subjective Element as the Expression of Acceptance of a Customary Rule

In the *Nicaragua* case, the Court considered the acceptance of an alleged customary rule by State(s) as proof of the subjective element.[18] In the *Fisheries Jurisdiction* case, the Court implied the subjective element in the same manner.[19]

In the Right of Passage case, the Court seemingly acknowledged the subjective element when it references the concept of practice:

> "...accepted by them as regulating their relations..." "...accepted as law by the parties..."[20]

In the *Lotus* case, the Court mentioned "usages generally accepted as expressing principles of law."[21] And once more, the Court, in the US Diplomatic and Consular Staff case, noted that the Vienna Convention "... state principles and rules... accepted throughout the world by nations of all creeds, cultures and political complexions."[22]

8. The Subjective Element as a Recognition of a Customary Rule

In the *Fisheries Jurisdiction* case, the Court used this concept when it asserted that "...reasonable regard must be had to such traditional rights by the coastal State, in accordance with the generally recognized principles embodied in Article 2 of the High Seas Convention."[23] The same term is used by the Court in the Opinion on *Reservations to Genocide Convention*: "...the principles underlying the Convention are principles which are recognized by civilized nations as binding on States, even without any conventional obligation."[24]

Analysis of the Court's Formulations

Items one, two, and three primarily deal with the same question: the subjective element as a belief regarding the legal relationship that constitutes a customary norm. As previously noted, the Court reduced the subjective element to one or both elements of this legal relation, within the context of the three possibilities that were analyzed. In utilizing the legal concepts of right and duty, the Court not only established the legal character of customary rule at hand, but also the existence of the norm itself. One scholar asserted that the legal right "is, like the legal duty, the legal norm in relation to a certain individual, designated by the norm itself."[25] The subjective element, being characterized in this manner, provides a clear guideline for the identification of customary rules as legal rules, which makes it very different from other types of social norms. Hans Kelsen asserts that, because of the social characteristic of legal norms, every right held by one individual calls for a duty to be imposed upon another person.[26] A jurisprudential debate surrounds this premise. Some commentators suggest that although every legal right imposes a corresponding legal duty, in-depth discussion on this matter often does not reveal this.[27] Alan White argues against the proposition that every legal right corresponds to a legal duty and vice versa.[28]

This discussion gets even more complex if you consider the possibility of the various meanings or practical applications assigned to the terms *right* and *duty*, and different types of legal relations that exist between these terms. There are even challenges to the structure of legal systems. One leading authority suggests that legal rules are not the only guidelines present in the domestic legal system; there must be attention given to legal principles and policies that are different from legal rules that affect the degree of what constitutes legal duties and/or rights established by legal principles.[29] But, this goes beyond the scope or approach that the Court uses since it uses a simpler methodology when it comes to connecting the concepts of legal rights and legal duties with the subjective element.

The requirement for defining the relationship between legal right and correlative duty (as expressed by item 1 above) could be for a simple reason. Most cases in which a legal relation was described generally involved bilateral or regional customs. One could attempt to use this perspective as a logical development of a specific legal regime created by such customs. In other words, the circle of participants is limited, and all of them are involved in the practice. Therefore, customs similar to these are more individualized and measurable: A State is endowed with rights and obligations that affect its legal relations with other States, and these rights and obligations do not necessarily have to be *erga omnes* obligations, which brings to mind the notion of strict mutuality.

The way the Court considered the legal relationship involves how it perceived the practice to which the customary rule refers and the way the contending States either applied or dismissed the existence of this norm. In all cases, one party invokes a legal rule which gives it the right to act in a certain way, while the other State is obligated not to impede the exercise of this right. With the exception of the Asylum case, there was no mention of other States having the same rights (based on the principle of reciprocity). Undoubtedly, the positive acts involved in the practices analyzed were performed exclusively by States that alleged the existence of a right: the other party to the dispute did not adopt the same course of behavior. In essence, these cases indicate that there is a connection between the specific features of international practice and the type of legal relationship that defines it. It is uncertain whether defining the legal relation this way makes much of a difference when the evidence is put to practical use. In essence, the Court can determine the legal rule, along with the subjective element, by identifying only one element. When the Court does this, the other element is automatically determined.

In instances where the Court found the subjective element correlates with the legal obligation established by the custom rule (item 2 above), it followed the opinion of various scholars.[30] In legal theory concerning domestic legal systems, the concept of *legal obligation* has been considered important when defining a legal rule. One writer noted that "the statement that someone has or is under an obligation does indeed imply the existence of a rule."[31] It is uncertain whether the Court considered legal obligation as the single factor in the legal relation when it comes to disputing a legal rule. Historically, commentators have criticized the notion of a single element when it comes to discerning customary rules.[32] This opposition notes that the notion of *opinio juris* has only an indirect and limited role in the acquisition of customary rights, and that this role is to be understood from the perspective of "States affected by the exercise of the right in question."[33]

The precept of legal positivism mandates that law generally has been described as commands, orders, duties, and sanctions. From Hans Kelsen's perspective, there is a fundamental relationship between the concepts of sanctions and legal duty since a duty can only be characterized when it is associated with a *threatened evil* or sanction.[34] According to Kelsen's analysis, sanction presupposes a legal obligation, so far as its practical application is conditional upon the occurrence of a breach of duty (i.e., non-compliance with obligation).[35] His perspective on sanctions provided an objective standard when it comes to defining a legal obligation or legal rule.

The application of this proposition to the international legal system suggests, for customary legal theory, that the existence or not of sanctions in their multifaceted forms is the real test of a legal rule. This applies whether the rules are conventional or customary in origin. Some scholars have noted that while this doctrine of subjective element inherently has flaws, it does have some validity.[36] Paul Guggenheim, a renowned scholar of international law, states that "for there to be custom, the conduct must be carried out in a constant and effective manner; it is also necessary that the violation be likely to be followed by a sanction."[37]

Within this context, the subjective element could be considered as the international practice at hand, reflecting a legal norm because behavior or actions that do not conform invite the remedial action of sanctions. In short, the subjective element could be defined as obligatory international practice fortified by the existence of sanctions. However, there are problems with this notion. In the first place, using the notion of sanctions to convey the subjective element could lead to other social rules using their version of sanctions when States are not in compliance. To address this problem, a definition of what comprises a *legal sanction* needs to be devised. Kelsen's definition, which states that legal sanctions are those remedial actions attached to a legal rule by the international legal system, is a functional definition.[38]

A second problem involving using the sanction criterion is that even within the domain of sanctions (which are applied due to the errant behavior or failure to uphold international standards), a wide range of sanctions may be applied, ranging from political, economic, or diplomatic sanctions. It is known that, for instance, sanctions applied by political or economic means are generally motivated and justified for political purposes regardless of whether the targeted State failed its international obligations. Sanctions that support ideological principles or a specific socio-economic system are not a rare phenomenon in the global sphere. What then can be done to separate these cases? Even when a legal obligation is breached by a State and sanctions are applied via political or economic means, without the aid of an effective objective authority empowered to ascertain *erga omnes*, the action taken may be viewed as a mere political expediency.

Hart notes that the seminal features of a legal obligation are that it is supported by explicit "social pressure brought to bear upon those who deviate" from an international obligation. While he lacks clarity in his explanation, he does give it substance when he refers to "physical sanctions," "insistence on performance," and "demand for conformity."[39] Another characteristic that Hart notes is the belief that a legal obligation is important because it serves as a focal point when it comes to maintaining international relations.[40] If the importance of a legal rule is the central part of legal obligation, it is not the only one. Legal obligations on issues that have far less weight do exist. Hart further asserts that the conduct it requires may "conflict with what the person who owes the duty may wish to do."[41] The one central fact that stands out is that legal obligations may cause States to sacrifice their own interests. As Hart so eloquently put it: "the standing possibility of conflict between obligation or duty and interest is, in all societies, among the truisms of both lawyer and moralist."[42]

A comprehensive examination of some interpretations regarding the concept of legal obligation shows the controversy that surrounds it. Hart suggests that the notion of obligation may serve as an empirical substitute for subjective ideas of *belief, fears*, or *motive*.[43] Hans Kelsen came to a completely different conclusion. He applied a psychological element (the fear of the repercussions that sanctions may cause).[44] Kelsen's main focus was commitment to a clinical definition of legal rules. He noted: "the statement that an individual is legally obliged to certain behaviors is an assertion about the contents of a legal norm and not about any actual events, especially not about the mental state of the obliged individual."[45] To bolster his argument, Kelsen referenced two examples: the notion that ignorance of law does not exempt from obligation, and the fact that norms are given retroactive force.[46]

Hart offers an entirely different analysis. He suggests that the external aspect of rules, what he calls "observable regularities of behaviors," does not define exactly how rules apply and function in the lives of those subject to them. He asserts that, instead of relying on the external aspect, the most important feature of a legal rule should lie in a "critical reflective attitude to certain patterns of behavior as a common standard."[47] Of course, like other elements of the law, there is a level of subjectivity involved. What Hart attempts to do is to apply some objective criteria by asserting that the internal aspects of rules are formulated within the context of "criticism, demands for conformity, and acknowledgements that such criticism and demands are justified."[48] While these criteria are significant, alone, none of them are fully acceptable. Hart's observations are relevant because he highlights the internal aspects and objectivity of a legal rule, but his analysis still invites subjectivity. Kelsen's framework provides a more objective baseline for identification and the definition of a legal obligation.

While an overview of the general theory of legal obligation has been conducted, there must be a detailed and comprehensive examination of an international legal obligation. Oscar Schachter argues that connecting the definition of obligatory legal norms with the legal process is paramount. An obligatory legal norm is said to exist when two conditions are met. In the first instance, the legal process which creates the obligation must fulfill some requisites, such as formulations of initial prescription, authority of law-makers, adherence to proper law-making procedures, willingness to respect and enforce the prescription, and communication of the requirement to the audience it is aimed at.

Secondly, once these conditions are met, the response of the target audience comes in two phases: (1) it has to perceive the prescription as authoritative in nature, and (2) likely to be complied with in the future to some substantial degree.[49] Schachter notes that an international legal obligation is established when the legal process fulfills some conditions, and States consider the prescription as effective and authoritative. If this proposition suggests that a legal obligation is one that derives from the normal operating mechanism of the legal process, then it is little more than a keen awareness of the obvious. It seems to rely on the old guidelines embraced by the traditional positivistic school of thought. This school of thought centers on the belief that the legal pedigree of a rule is determined by whether it was developed through the formal process of law.[50] Its usage depends on how well the customary process is defined and identified, since States (the target audience) must know how to identify a regular legal process and understand how it operates before they can judge or perceive whether the prescription is truly authoritative and effective and could be considered a legal obligation. The second part of the definition does not seem to elaborate on the subject. To rely on how effective the prescription is as a central mechanism seems unnecessary, since a non-legal social rule may also likely be complied with in future international relationships.

The notion that a customary norm and the subjective element can be expressed in terms of a legal right (item *three* above) highlights some interesting points. As noted previously, in general, every legal right correlates to a legal obligation.

From this perspective, when only a legal right in isolation is being applied, the subjective element may still be defined by referring to the legal obligation in two ways: (a) from the perspective that there exists a legal obligation which corresponds to a legal right, or (b) from the perspective that the State which has the right to act in a certain manner is not under the legal obligation to adhere to the legal obligation.

As mentioned above, the Court decided to apply a general notion of legal right in its approach. It did not consider the possibility that this notion might have diverse meanings and therefore express diverse legal circumstances or legal relationships. A legal right could mean a specific claim, privilege, or power. It is uncertain whether these distinctions would have had any impact on the Court's reasoning process.

In determining the existence of a legal right, more attention should be given to its practicality and not merely to its invocation. The way a legal right is exercised may invalidate its existence and the presence of the subjective element contained in the issue at hand. The *Right of Passage* case proves that this aspect is very important. In this case, the Court decided whether the alleged right of passage of armed forces, armed police, and ammunition was "permitted or exercised as a right". The Court ruled that "no right of passage in favor of Portugal involving a correlative obligation on India has been established in respect of armed forces, armed police, and ammunition."[51] When it came to the finding on the non-existence of the alleged right, two factors were considered relevant by the Court: the fact that the practice in question involved the principle of reciprocity, and the exercise of the right was predicated on the prior approval of the other State.[52]

To determine the existence of an alleged right by its practical use may prove to be problematic. One must consider that by its nature, a legal right is discretionary. This means that States that have a legal right to perform certain acts or behave in a specific manner are not obligated to do so: they act according to their discretion. As a result, there could be fewer instances of State practice to depend on. Additionally, in situations where the State fails to exercise its rights, the distinction between the discretionary use of a legal right and actions based upon political or economic expediency may become blurred.

The use by the Court of the concepts of legal right and legal obligation when it comes to ascertaining the subjective element is designed to determine the legal character of a specific rule. Strictly speaking, when the subjective element is expressed in this context, it serves an important function: to serve as a mechanism that makes a distinction between law and non-law. This notion of the subjective element is more representative of the concept of *lex lata*, which essentially means *law as it exists*. This may serve the Court well as a useful guide, but it also entails the complex nature of the subjective element.

In relation to items *seven* and *eight* above (acceptance and recognition), there is no determination that the Court used either expression to convey the notion of the subjective element. If these concepts were used differently from that of the subjective element, one could question the use of the subjective element (at least in situations where the other two concepts were used).

Characterizing the subjective element as a recognition of a given customary rule (item *8* above) involves a sociological analysis. It seems that connecting the legal or customary character of the rule to a factual state of affairs is predicated on answering the following question: what standards or international practices do the actors of the international system recognize as definitive customary rules at the given moment? Answering this question merely suggests that the actors believe that a customary rule exists within the international legal system. There is nothing stopping this perception from encompassing certain features of customary rules, such as their local, regional, or general character.

Recognition, Oscar Schachter suggests, does not imply an act of consensual acceptance.[53] This analysis is important because although some Justices of the Court have used the terms interchangeably (recognition and acceptance) in their opinions, a distinction can be made between the two concepts.[54] Logically, the recognition of a rule precedes its acceptance of the rule. Additionally, a description of the subjective element in terms of acceptance of the rule highlights a State's consent as the main criterion for its normative quality and existence. Whether the Court or individual Justices had this notion in mind is pure speculation. The opinions of the Court show a constant oscillation between consensual and non-consensual or objective justifications. This may be attributed to the flexible approach of the Court rather than to any doctrinal indifference.[55]

Item *four* above concerns the possibility of the Court making constructive use of the subjective element. In the instances cited in this item, the Court was not defining *opinio juris* as a way to uphold the validity of a custom. It used the phrase *customary international law* to specify the group of rules that is developed from a specific source. Why? The Court likely felt that there was a need to highlight the distinct nature of the legal opinion at hand, which concerned the recognition of a parallel operative or wholesale validity of a rule as it is expressed within the confines of customary international law. In short, the identification of a customary rule also means that the rule has a special characteristic. Paul Reuter applied a similar proposition to the subjective element. He suggests that since a rule of *jus cogens* originates from custom, the rule of *jus cogens* consists of a specific "kind of *opinio juris*... a kind of absolute" rule.[56] Item *5* needs no explanation. Its logical corollary is built upon the proposition that a rule has been identified and its contents are known.

The Court has addressed situations involving omissions (item *six* above), as this action relates to other States in a variety of ways. What is self-evident is the significant role of the subjective element in determining whether the omission was legally relevant, or whether the omission supports the notion of an established customary rule. Some commentators suggest that omission has been used to establish a deliberate act motivated by the existence of a customary rule.[57] When the subjective element is expressed in this manner, there is very little difference between omission and acceptance (which essentially reduces the subjective element to acceptance). This premise has a historical basis.[58] During situations of infrequent use, the subjective element takes on another form. In these cases, the subjective element may indicate a deliberate act(s) where a State is motivated by other reasons, such as the perception that the customary rule no longer applies or does not exist.

Evolutionary Developments in Customary International Law

As noted earlier, the description of the subjective element is presented in terms of case-law and relative canons, which only covers a specific area of customary rules: when the rules have fully developed. Doctrinally, various theoretical frameworks and scholarly examinations attempt to define the subjective element as it relates to the State and the customary process.

Theoretical Frameworks on the Subjective Element

Bin Cheng asserts that the subjective element is the most significant element in the development of a customary rule.[1] Thus, the customary process can function effortlessly by appealing to the subjective element. This could be accomplished when a State, either unilaterally or in agreement with other States, declares a new *opinio juris* regarding general international law on a specific issue.[2] Cheng notes that this is based on the premise of when and if the individual opinion of the States representing the prevailing view of the international community mirrors that of other States, which essentially establishes a general *opinio juris* and a general international norm.[3] He further suggests that the subjective element can be considered "the view held by, or that may be said, with effect opposable to that State, to be held by, a State as to what the law is"[4] or *lex lata* in more formal terms. The States accept that the norm is characterized as a legal term (and not merely social or moral precepts) and carries the obligation of legal rights.[5]

A cursory review would suggest that Cheng believes that a State may hold this position regardless of what stage the customary process is in. If he supports this premise, there would be little distinction between what the law is (*lex lata*) and what the law ought to be (*lex ferenda*). A distinction should be made when two different types of situations occur:

(a) when the new *opinio juris* applies to an issue that was at the time unregulated, and (b) when the new *opinio juris* involves a matter that falls under a previously established general rule of international law.

In both cases, which Cheng did not distinguish, it would be problematic for States that started a new practice to validate their conduct by appealing to a general customary rule that is already in existence. In a situation that falls under (b), the State concerned may be intentionally attempting to change the law by not adhering to its guidelines or would rely upon an incomplete or unclear analysis of the law.

Critical Analysis of Cheng's Examples

The descriptive example put forth by Cheng that falls under (b) seemingly invalidates this reasoning. For instance, take Cheng's comments regarding the Truman Proclamation and *opinio juris.* He asserted that the Truman Proclamation should be considered an *opinio juris* for the United States because "international law allows a coastal State to appropriate title to the natural resources of the adjacent continental shelf."[6] Did the United States explicitly use the concept of *opinio juris* to express its opinion or its desire that it would correspond to an international rule? This is highly unlikely. In the *North Sea* cases, the Court reasoned that it was the first development of the law on the issue.[7] Cheng concurs with the Court's reasoning. He notes that at the judicial level, the Truman Proclamation "would have been declared contrary to international law."[8] Cheng's comments here are revealing. He is essentially admitting that the State which articulates a new *opinio juris* is compelled to "naturally defend its innovation as a much better rule for international society as a whole."[9] This assertion seems to differ from the definition of the subjective element. The belief that an opinion of the law is "A" on a specific issue and a justification that it could be desirable to be "A" on the same issue is, without a doubt, a contradiction.

Cheng offers another instance that can be examined. This instance concerns Canada's extension of its territorial sea, in which the Canadian Government (in justifying this action) expressed its view that international law on this matter was "moving from the three to the twelve-mile limit."[10] What this meant was that the law was complicated and precarious but trending toward becoming settled law. It begs the question: how could this be considered Canada's opinion that general customary law at the time of Canada's actions could be deemed carrying out legal rights and duties *erga omnes*? This is only feasible if one takes the view that in cases where the law is complicated or unsettled, either course of action is permissible. However, Cheng's proposition would have to include endorsing the validity and application of the principle: what is not forbidden is allowed. His analysis of Canada's Arctic Waters Pollution Prevention Act is open to the same interpretation. Noting that Canada acknowledged that there was no law on the subject, Cheng characterized the Act as an *opinio juris* that "general international law permits a coastal State to extend its jurisdiction to the extent she has claimed for the purpose of preventing pollution."[11]

Alternative Perspective on Cheng's Framework

However, Cheng's theoretical framework is worthy of being viewed from a different perspective. In outlining his view of the international legal system, he asserts that the majority of international laws rest on the auto-interpretative level, where each State has a right to give its own interpretation of the law.[12] Since they are an integral part of the law-making process, States can act to implement changes to the law.[13] Cheng maintains that the "initial-error" hypothesis is not a part of the customary process.[14] When any State articulates a new *opinio juris*, it is irrelevant whether the state of the law correlates with what the State asserts. The most essential thing is whether other States will change or amend their legal opinion or not. Above, Cheng (in reference to the Truman Proclamation) noted that the United States had "clearly advanced a new rule of general international law," and this had been "a deliberate act due to no initial error."[15] According to Cheng's perspective, the customary process employs an auto-interpretative mechanism within the confines of international law, and in the developmental stages, the subjective element is a law-creating apparatus.

Cheng's constructive theoretical framework suggests that the definition of *opinio juris* needs some type of modification. Such discussion, as noted earlier, is more indicative of established customary norms rather than those that are in the developmental process. When the majority of the international community shares the same legal opinion, and a customary norm is established, then the subjective element mirrors the definition that Cheng put forth.

D'Amato's Claim-Oriented Perspective

If Cheng's constructive interpretation is correct, then it intersects with the theoretical framework put forth by Anthony D'Amato. D'Amato asserts that international law is a "process of relative persuasion" whereby "the better of two conflicting claims prevails."[16] The subjective element, as it applies to D'Amato's theoretical framework, must be viewed from the claim-oriented perspective. He defines it as an "articulation of a rule of international law."[17] In a claim situation that engenders disputes, various contradictory rules may be expressed simultaneously by different States. According to D'Amato, the customary process involves applying precedents based upon expressed rules, which in turn mature into a customary norm.[18] A customary norm is established once some States follow it out of a sense of legal obligation, and other States find "it difficult to challenge the practice."[19] When an expressed rule is demonstrated by the actions of a State, the other rules remain "in the realm of speculation."[20] The active nature of the subjective element is an overarching theme in Cheng and D'Amato's theoretical frameworks.

Critiques of D'Amato's Theory

D'Amato's proposition has encountered numerous challenges, specifically involving the definition of the subjective element and its role in the development of a customary rule. D'Amato notes that "theorizing in international law requires the drawing of generalizations from a number of instances and in this sense is an inductive process." In his own words, his theory emphasizes "functional, as opposed to the conceptualistic aspects of the theory." In short, he supports the notion that empirical knowledge can give rise to a better understanding of international law.

However, this perspective can be challenged. On a logical and classification level, analysis of the material furnished by empirical reality implies that a working framework is in place. It's correct to determine, by using the inductive method, the content of law (but this method does not apply to ascertaining the conception of the law). One scholar of historical significance stated: "To say that the concept of law exists only in what is given by experience is to deny a principle while relying on its results, because law could not be determined if its concept was not first averred and applied."[21] Karl Popper has also criticized the use of the inductive method to infer universal statements.[22]

D'Amato also fails to understand that any realities associated with State practice cannot possibly start from a conceptual *tabula rasa*, as reflected in some of the conclusions he draws. Some of his hypotheses come from a picture entirely different from what actually happens in the customary process. For instance, it is difficult to accept D'Amato's suggestion that States express a general customary rule based on one or even a few precedents. In expressing a general customary rule, States do not rely on one precedent; on the contrary, they articulate a number of precedents to indicate that a general trend has developed. The central problem associated with a claim-conflict-based theory is that it tends to be contextually bilateral, and the proposition that D'Amato put forth follows along these lines. It completely disregards the multilateral development of customary international law.

His theory does not explore the justification presented by States when they commence a new practice. Basically, the subjective element is an expression of a rule. State practice indicates, in contrast to D'Amato's perspective, that States who partake in the developmental stages of the customary process offer precedents as well as legal and non-legal rationalizations for their conduct.

States not only proffer a specific rule, but they also generally present their behavior and actions in the best legal light possible. These rationalizations may be a definitive factor when it comes to the development of a customary rule.[23]

Thirlway's Perspective: Opinio Necessitatis

Addressing the issue of rationalization put forth by States, H.W.A. Thirlway offers a different perspective. He built his proposition around the concept of *opinio juris sive necessitatis*, which suggests that States initiate new practices under the umbrella of *opinio necessitatis* (the practice is *necessary as law*).[24] Thirlway also argues that opinio necessitatis is adequate to create a customary rule of law.[25] Exactly what he means by "*necessary as law*" is unclear. He cannot mean that the practice is made essential by reason of existing law because this would be no different between his view and the view expounded by the pre-existing rule school, a school of thought he had previously dismissed. Perhaps he means the philosophical aspects when he suggested this definition. If so, the expression of "necessary as law" would mean that States believe that the new practice needs to be law. In other words, it would need to become mandatory *erga omnes* as a general customary rule. But even in this instance, there is still the question: is it his subjective opinion or does it have aspirational overtones? If it is aspirational, the legal opinion at hand would constitute an expression on the desirability of the rule, mirroring the concept of *de lege ferenda* (what the law should be). Classic scholars, such as Francisco Suarez, have previously noted the significance that intent has when it comes to creating custom.[26] Concerning the creation of a *binding custom* as opposed to a custom of fact or practical usage, Suarez believes that it is important that the participants intend to establish this type of custom. While this framework reflects the reality that States developing a new practice may intend to bring the new custom rule into reality, it does very little to justify their conduct in doing so.

Social Necessity and the Law

A further discussion as to why States believe that the new practice needs to evolve into law can be summarized. By emphasizing the word "necessary," Thirlway also emphasized that the new practice was essential. Some commentators suggest that if the law is indicative of a social necessity, the State, which starts a new practice, could justify it on the basis of this concept and mandate that it needs to become law.[27] Some Judges agree with this proposition and have supported it in the opinions of the ICJ.[28] This argument is based on the notion that necessity helps facilitate the law. Notwithstanding the circularity of this argument – the law is necessary and necessity produces the law – it may be asserted that although what is necessary may indeed turn out to be the law, not all necessities inherently produce the law. There is always the argument that there are various kinds or distinctions between types of necessity. For instance, there could be absolute necessities, and there could be relative necessities.

An analogy could be made between the concepts of necessity and utility. Historically, some scholars have noted that there is a correlation between legal rights and utility, and used this to develop a concept of the law.[29] Causality seems to be a contributing factor in this argument concerning social necessity. Law (consequent) is found upon the basis of social necessity (antecedent). The fallacy of this approach is that it does not explain the beginning or the end of this proposition. For example, there should be a cause for this social necessity and so on. Besides, on a practical level, identifying a social necessity is a subjective endeavor.

However, questions arise as to whether there is a need for social necessity or what actually causes social necessity. What is really of interest is that States apply it to validate their practices. But then, how can it be ascertained whether the necessity that is applied really exists or is only a strategic mechanism used to establish the rule? Well, it is irrelevant how a social necessity is characterized because other States will either respond to it in a positive or negative manner, which will justify the claim that is put forth. There are other challenges that could be made to this perspective. First, upon in-depth analysis, that in the formative stages of the customary process, the concept of social necessity is not uniform, which facilitates contradictory practices by various States. States could contend that since the practice exists, it is a necessity. Another problem is that even on a theoretical level, there is a common belief or perspective of social necessity and a perceived way of meeting this social need, which could result in non-uniformity. State practice also indicates that States generally are concerned with their own specific needs, which may be counterproductive to the common need of the customary process. For example, in the *Right of Passage* case, Portugal referenced the subjective element as a social need to justify the existence of an established customary rule that only served its interests.[30] Portugal asserted that the passage between Damao and the enclaves was "absolutely" a necessity.[31] India contested this claim.[32]

The Pre-Existing Rule School

This author would be remiss if the pre-existing rule school of thought was not examined. Fundamentally, this school of thought supports the notion that a customary practice, even during the developmental stages, reflects a pre-existing legal rule. Because of this, general practices would not be considered a law-making factor, but only a revelation of the law. This school of thought is heavily criticized since it inherently denies that the customary process could be a formal source of law. This was the central argument used by the members of the International Law Commission to contest Hudson's proposition that one of the requirements of a custom is that the practice must correlate with prevailing international law.[33]

Considering the International Law Commission's objections, Hersch Lauterpacht addressed this issue by noting that in the developmental stages of the customary process, there is an element of obligation that may not be necessarily legal in nature because the conduct could be influenced by "duties of neighborliness, reasonableness, and accommodation."[34] This notion is diametrically opposite to the strict pre-existing rule because it offers non-legal guidelines for newly established practices.

The Relationship between the Subjective Element and State Practice

Both scholars and the Court recognize two elements in a customary rule: the subjective element and the material element (State practice). These elements are addressed and approached differently according to whether they are a component of a customary norm or fulfill a contributing role to the development of a customary norm. Historically, some scholars have noted that the subjective element is an *ex post facto* element of a customary rule, while some see the subjective element as preceding the material element.[1] This goes far beyond a simple disagreement about the specific order or time frame in which these elements appear. The main reason that a greater exclusive role is given to one element over the other is because of the perspective that one has of international law.[2] While one of the elements has a contributive role in the development of a rule, the other is characterized as evidence that the rule has already been developed.

As noted earlier, both elements are interrelated. The question whether one or the other element is prior in time is immaterial because both elements are present in each stage of the customary process. The subjective element is an integral part of every phase of a customary process, and not only when the rule has fully developed. A good example is provided by this illustration: human actions are juridically relevant to a subjective will. Thus, this allows for external manifestation coupled with internal motivation. As Rudolf Ihering succinctly puts it: "acting and acting with a purpose are synonymous."[3] In essence, an act of a State should be considered an expression of its intent and will.

The Subjective Element by Another Name?

The capacity of the subjective element is multifaceted. It could be used as a guideline for identifying the law, justifying a particular action or behavior, and creating new rules. When a State specifies an *opinio juris*, it typifies three things:

1. A State's position concerning the state of the law on a specific issue;
2. A State's perspective as to the legality of its practice in comparison to the existing law (whether it correlates with the law); and
3. A State's perspective regarding *opinio juris* as it pertains to the practice of other States.

These three factors are present whenever an *opinio juris* is evidenced, but differ in composition according to the state of the customary process and/or the specific custom that is being addressed.

Therefore, it is essential to review four possible situations that could occur in a customary process:

Situation (A): Where an established practice is unchallenged by a contradictory practice.

Situation (B): Where a new practice addresses an issue previously unregulated by international law.

Situation (C): Where State(s) intentionally develop a new practice, which is inconsistent with or conflicts with an existing rule.

Situation (D): Where two different groups initiate two conflicting practices that entail different customary rules.

In **Situation A**, an *opinio juris* expressed by a State should refer to its view that international law is established on the question in the form of a customary rule, which the State is actively or passively involved in, and correlates with customary international law. The State and other States should have legal rights and obligations derived from the customary rule, and their own practice is legal and consistent with international law. Any dissident practice constitutes a violation of the customary rule, and the practice and the *opinio juris* of the generality of States are resolved in the same manner.

Situation B happens in those cases where new developments reveal a new phase of State actions that are not regulated by international law. The first activities in outer space are a good illustration of new practices and developments previously unregulated by international law.[4] When a State demonstrates or reveals *opinio juris* as it relates to a practice, the practice should explicitly show that international law is silent on the matter, and that the action corresponds or is permitted by international law.[5] Any course of action taken by other States is also permissible until international law clarifies the issue, and that other States hold the same *opinio juris*. It is feasible that the State which commences the new practice understands that some rules of international law are applicable to new practices by similarity, in which case the *opinio juris* would maintain that, while international law lacks clarity in order to fully address the new issue or practice, in view of the rules that are already applicable, the issue or practice corresponds with international law.

Regarding **Situation C**, the State(s) that initiated the new practice could never be regarded as having an *opinio juris* in the sense of the two definitions above. Unless there is a misperception of what the law means when it comes to the issue at hand, it should support the notion that its practice, while inconsistent with existing international law on the issue, was justified on a universal basis. This justification may be supported by some extra-legal mechanism, such as social necessity, self-preservation, insufficiency of current law, or reasonableness of a State's practice or its actions. For example, in the Preamble of the Truman Proclamation on the Continental Shelf, it is asserted, inter alia, that the exercise of jurisdiction over the continental shelf is necessary, "reasonable and just," and compelled by a sense of "self-protection."[6] With this in mind, States could still apply other legal rules to support their arguments. States could assert that the international legal system supports changes in the law through new or diverging practices, provided that these changes do not violate *jus cogens* rules or other standardized norms used to maintain equity and fairness in the international community.

In **Situation D**, the international practice on the issue suggests ambiguity.[7] It suggests that there are two or more diverging practices, each being followed by States in a uniform manner. International law is ambiguous in the sense that rules do not operate in a legal vacuum, or that there are two or more conflicting rules regarding the same matter. It is doubtful that any State from either group implements this first interpretation, instead of applying its own version of the rule. Thus, taking into consideration the second interpretation, States that pursue or follow the more recent practice imply that:

1. International law is unclear or unsettled on the issue, which allows the action to be permissible;
2. Its own actions or practices correspond with international law;
3. Their actions or practices correspond with regional custom;
4. That it and other States possess legal rights and/or obligations derived from customary international law;
5. Any deviation from the practice amounts to a violation of the rule; and
6. That the practice and the *opinio juris* of other States are resolved in the same manner.

There is a possibility that those States that pursue a new practice apply *opinio juris* in the same manner as described in **Situation A**. It is also likely that States which adhere to the old rule will continue to hold an *opinio juris* similar to the one outlined in **Situation A**. Nevertheless, they could also demonstrate that *opinio juris, inter se,* supports their customary rule.

Hypothetically, a State can hold more than one type of *opinio juris*. There may also be a universal expression of *opinio non-juris* – the belief that a previously established customary rule has little effectiveness or validity due to neglect, disuse, or instant abrogation, which leaves it in a legal vacuum. An individual demonstration of *opinio non-juris* suggests that the practice is detached from any legal rule, cannot produce a legal effect, and is only performed by the discretion of the State(s), for political reasons, or by direct or collateral extra-legal reasons.[8]

Chapter VI
The Customary Process: A Theoretical and Practical Examination

Examining the nature of the customary process is both extensive and very complex. It is very important to study the actions of States within the international system and what legal effects may arise from their behavior. There are various points to address and interactions to examine to ascertain how the customary process operates.

State Actions and the International System

The way the social and structural environment of the international system influences the overall behavior of States defines how the customary process is viewed. Legal considerations, coupled with how and when to follow a course of action, affect the States' final decision to move forward. To ascertain how a given State reacts or behaves, there must be an analysis of the restraints and influences that affect its behavior.

Social Factors and State Behavior

States react to various situations in complicated ways. States generally use rationale when pursuing their objectives and interests. However, their behavior is shaped by a multifaceted set of social factors. Social factors that often influence a State's action are determined by the social condition of the State. In other words, how States interact with other States is a contributing factor to a State's behavior.

Action taken by a State that engenders an international issue creates a ripple effect that is felt by other States. In essence, as noted by the modified Binomial Theorem model below, any action by a State may give rise to a reaction by other States. The Binomial Theorem traditionally describes the algebraic expansion of powers of a binomial. This modified application demonstrates the mathematical relationship where the sum of State Action (SA) directed toward State B (SB) equals State Reaction (SR), illustrating how actions in the international system generate measurable responses.

$$\sum_{SA}^{SB} = SR$$

This mutual and/or reciprocal action is better known as interaction. Of course, a single act does not completely define the concept of interaction. It must consist of some type of dynamic element, an element where a reaction to an act compels a reaction to that reaction. Bilateral relationships are representative of dynamic interaction. Essentially, States in bilateral relationships are mutually responding and adjusting to each other's behavior. Most acts involving interaction do not have to concern the same issue or be of the same nature. For example, State X claims that a specific area adjacent to its coast is now under its jurisdiction and sovereignty. State Y may deploy naval forces in the area in order to secure continued use, by exploitation, of the natural resources by its nationals. This illustration indicates that one of the States has two different (but related) types of action.

Action or a specific behavior is more likely than not to get a reaction from other States. Deciding how to respond to an act is based on various factors.

Expectations

One leading expert noted that decisions are predicated on policymakers' anticipation of decisions made at the same or some future point in time by other actors.[1] A State that is seeking to achieve its objectives knows that it is likely to gain a positive reaction from other States if their behavior or acts correspond to what the other States expect it to be. Of course, there is the possibility that the State will follow a course of conduct that would manifest negative reactions from other States.

The expectations of other States regarding the conduct of other States may involve a multitude of factors. For example, these expectations could be defensible by an international norm that (according to the State) regulates the subject matter to which the act pertains. Thus, a State expects another State to act in conformity with the standards of international law rather than risk the costs of derogation from international law.[2] Expectations as to a specific State's behavior may also come from a previous pattern of behavior that is acknowledged by other States.[3] A State's past actions also influence expectations, since other States may believe that the behavior in question will continue. Expectations are inherently a part of both sides of the relationship. It is rational to assume that in reacting to a particular act or behavior, a State takes into consideration the expectations of the acting State when it decides to react. For example, a reacting State may adjust its negative reaction because it believes that a stronger response would cause the other State to take even stronger or disproportionate counter-measures.

State Preferences and Interactions in International Relations

Preferences

A State's desire for the best possible outcomes during interaction with another State represents its *preferences*. Each State in the interstate relationship has its own set of preferences. It is safe to say that a State which is inclined to perform an act will do so within the parameters of its own preferences. Historical antecedents exemplify this. During the years of colonial America, the political leaders of the colonies decided that all commercial interactions with foreign countries would be done in the spirit of collecting revenue and protecting the colony's merchants. This revenue enhancement and protectionist policy came under the umbrella of the Declaration of Colonial Rights of 1774.[1] This Declaration stated that "the regulation of external commerce" was established "for the purpose of securing the commercial advantages of the whole empire."[2] Later, as an established country, the United States' Constitution, under Article I, Section 8, Clause 3, authorized the encouragement and protection of manufactures, and permitted the application of duties on goods, wares, and imports.[3] Hence, some States have codified their preferences when interacting with other States.

The Role of Attributes in Interactions

Attributes play a significant role in interactions when it comes to determining the impact of States' behavior. The expectations and preferences of those States whose interests will be more affected by a State's behavior or actions are dictated by the decision-making process, substance of the behavior and action, and the form of the conduct. For example, when an act is to give rise to an interaction which involves States that are politically and economically unified, as in the case with the European Union, the acting State must consider the expectations and preferences of the States with which it deals before carrying out a specific act. Likewise, reactions from those States to an act performed by one of them should be weighed carefully in light of the expectations of the acting State. For instance, during the Falkland War, the European Economic Community maintained a common reaction to the actions taken by Argentina, as the economic embargo demonstrates.[4]

This premise applies to the expectations and preferences of industrially powerful States as well, especially to those States that use their influence to coerce less powerful States to make unfavorable decisions. More influential and powerful States have a greater sphere of global influence and generally are more directly affected by the acts of other States.

Structural Effects

Structural effects have their own set of influences that must be taken into consideration. The international system is established and arranged in a manner where units fall under an ordering principle, with varying capabilities. These units exert their own influence upon other States' behaviors in a variety of ways.

Differentiated Values for Behaviors

The degree of power that a State holds can be measured in terms of the attributes that influence its relationship with other States. Better known as a social factor, it involves the dissemination of power amongst States and how this distribution impacts State-to-State interaction.

The dissemination of power amongst States entails differing levels of capabilities. In contemporary times, power is seemingly held by a few States. The more power that a State wields, the more its actions and behavior influence other States' actions and behavior. If the capabilities and power of the States were evenly distributed, then there would be equity in the legal and political process. But this does not reflect the realities of the geo-political system. The only way to balance this inequality is by forming units or groups of States for the attainment of a common objective. This may not always be beneficial, because powerful States may work together for their own common objectives.

Decentralized Interactions

Anarchy represents the structure of the international system. That is, States are juridically equal, and there is no concept of hierarchy between them nor a superior authority. Because the international system is organized in an anarchical manner, interactions between States are voluntary and decentralized. Because of this, States can and should correlate their actions when their interests converge in order to achieve a common objective. Even in instances where interests conflict, a cooperative effort generally serves the interests of the parties involved.

However, decentralized interactions entail a certain level of uncertainty, especially if the interactions are uncoordinated. While various States pursue an objective either individually or through bilateral interaction to reach their goals, they could still encounter a result that is altogether different from that which the State originally intended. For example, suppose that State *X* is seeking to protect its security interests and is facing a predicament: it's located in a region of great political upheaval and feels that its neighbors are a potential threat to its sovereignty, its territorial integrity, and its political stability. In addition to this dilemma, State *X* believes that the military imbalance in the region has been shifting in favor of its neighbors. To counter this, State X strengthens its military infrastructure to restore the balance of power and to deter the possibility of threats. Its fundamental objective is to increase its own security while enhancing its political influence in the region. Yet, it is more likely than not that its neighbors will feel insecure by State *X's* new acquisition of arms and will proceed to respond by increasing and strengthening their own military. As a result, State *X* and its neighbors would carry on an arms race, yet they both will continue to feel insecure. Thus, the original objectives of the parties would eventually be displaced or supplanted by the final results.

Behavior Determinants and the Formation of Rules

Social factors and structural influences both determine and explain State actions and behavior. In essence, the State does not act in a vacuum; it generally acts and behaves in a complex manner in response to its social and environmental structure. As functional elements, social and structural factors play a definitive role when it comes to a State deciding when to act, how to react, and how their actions reverberate throughout the international legal system. But do these factors explain or clarify the emergence of a specific pattern of State behavior? Understanding the answer to this question throws light on the formation of a general practice that plays a significant role in the development of a custom.

Social factors and structural influences sometimes explain why a particular action is taken and why a specific reaction to that action occurs. However, they provide an inadequate reason why some States follow the same course of action that a particular State has previously engaged in. In other words, they fail to explain why the reaction to the action is positive. Robert Axelrod gives some clarity to this process under the evolutionary principle.[5] This principle suggests that strategies that are "relatively effective" will be used more in the future than less effective strategies.[6] This principle seems to be more applicable to social environments than to other environments. Within the international system, the evolutionary principle supports the notion that States generally mimic the conduct of another State when the conduct has been successful. Success, in this context, means that the objectives and interests of the State were achieved by the performance of a specific action. The evolutionary principle assumes that the objectives and interests satisfied by the conduct or action that is being mimicked are similar to both States. In conclusion, the action and behavior of a State are predicated on social factors and structural effects. Once the conduct is successfully performed, it may be readily adopted by other States through the application of the evolutionary principle, which in turn helps develop a legal or social norm.

The Legal Influence of State Acts and Interactions

There is a difference between positive and negative acts: Positive acts describe actual acts or behavior, while negative acts refer to legally relevant omissions. This difference can be made between a single act and a combination of acts. A single act is an act performed only once by a single entity, like an act of Congress. A combination of acts consists of a series of acts regarding the same issue that is performed by one or more States, either as a cooperative effort or not. Because composite acts involve a sense of continuity, they could be understood within the context of behavior or conduct. State practice pertaining to maritime issues, for example, has shown that many maritime issues have been applied by a combination of acts involving the three main branches of a State's government. Legislative enactments are generally followed by executive edicts and then by judicial measures concerning the application of the claim and its enforcement.[7] There is also the distinction between an act within the context of it being definite or indefinite. A definite act is validated when it explicitly addresses a specific State, while an indefinite act is inherently directed toward all States, that is, *erga omnes*.

There are two ways that a State may produce legal effects: it may affect the general nature of the law on a given issue, and it may dictate the inner workings of a specific legal relationship. For clarification, a legal relationship consists of a situation where interaction is regulated by international law. International law regulates interaction by developing and determining the rights and obligations that apply to a specific situation.

It is by the influence of those two types of legal effects that new customary norms are created and existing customary norms are abrogated or altered. These effects are interrelated since they are produced by States' acts and contribute to the same result. They differ from one another by the fact that established legal rules precede the general influence that a specific act may have on the nature of the law. When acknowledging the legal effects of a State act, one is also acknowledging that those effects are only produced when combined with other States' acts and reactions.

Establishing a specific legal relationship is the immediate effect of a State act. When States commence a new practice, new legal relationships generally are established, but the legal basis for it may not be engendered in a customary rule. However, the customary process evolves along with these new legal relationships. The customary rule that is eventually created by the customary process will reflect the legal rights and obligations found in the new legal relationships.

State Acts and Legal Relationships

State acts that facilitate a new customary process are generally embodied in new legal claims. With that in mind, there is a need to define the concept of a legal claim.

The Concept of Legal Claims and the Customary Process

The notions of legal claims and legal rights have always been interrelated. However, there are various interpretations detailing the relationship between the two concepts. As it applies to the customary process, States have a legal claim while possessing a legal right. Because there is an established customary rule, a legal claim may be equated with a legal right. In fact, it would seem improper to say that a State is making a legal claim to a right which has already been generally recognized as established.[1]

If the exercise of the right to which the State(s) have a claim is abridged by another State, then every claimant State would be entitled to enforce its claim or at least its right to do so. If the generally recognized right is ever obstructed by a specific State, then the claimant State does not have to make a claim to the existence of the right: it can simply enforce its claim.

In order to better understand this premise, one could also define the concept of legal claim by reference to the definition of the other related concept: that of legal right. In essence, in a customary process which has reached the final stages, every State has a legal right in the sense of possessing a legal claim which is recognizable and enforceable. Because of this inherent right, such right is also comprised of the right to claim the enforcement or the acknowledgment of the duty to ensure that this right is unimpeded.

During the developmental period of the customary process, States do not have a legal claim (in the same sense as it is described above) but make a legal claim. A legal claim asserted at this point either refers to an alleged existence and possession of a legal right or to the desirability of the existence and possession of a legal right.[2]

When a State puts forth a legal claim under the guise of asserting a legal right to do so, this does not indicate that the right asserted actually exists or that it really possesses this right. That is a claim that can be manipulative. Actually, this sort of claim is commonly made to attempt to create a right, and the State that makes it knows that it does not even exist. Of course, the claimant State will not admit this, but this lack of admission does not negate the fact that there is a real discrepancy between what a State claims and what really exists.

A comment can be made on the legal claim as it pertains to a legal right. The State that asserts this type of claim knows and acknowledges that the right in question does not exist, and it does not have this right. This type of claim falls under the category of *de lege ferenda* because it represents an attempt to change the law.

State acts that facilitate the development of legal relationships generally entail claims that are inherent to the customary process. A legal claim represents intention, or a conscious attitude designed to bring about a desired result, namely, the general recognition and implementation of a given right. It consists of asserting the existence or desirability of a new right *erga omnes*, either with an intent to oppose an existing right or not.

It is noteworthy that in the initial stage of the customary process, States are inclined to put forth a legal claim to a right which clearly does not derive from any bilateral or multilateral agreements or from custom (either general, bilateral, or regional). With this in mind, it could be concluded that States are essentially claiming a new right.

It is also worthy noting that although the claimant State is aware that the claimed right does not exist when it makes the claim, it usually acts as though the right does exist. In this way, the claimed right(s) could be embodied in domestic legislation and enforced *erga omnes* by the claimant State. For example, in a diplomatic note sent to Japan in 1958, the Government of Mexico made it clear that it maintained the "validity and obligations *erga omnes*, of the provisions enforced in the Mexican legislation on the matter, establishing the width of the territorial sea of Mexico in 9 nautical..."[3]

This premise is supported by the fact that the successful enforcement and defense of a legal claim facilitates the development of the rule maintained by it. A result of this premise is that a legal claim is not confined within the parameters of mere words; it creates new avenues that differ from previously existing situations.

But when will legal claims develop into substantive legal rights? In the early stages of the customary process, legal claims may give rise to legal rights only when specific legal relationships are established within the parameters below. It is noteworthy that legal rights which arise out of legal relationships have no customary source, since *ex hypothesi* there is no established customary norm in the sense of the right claimed. As the customary norm evolves, States can have a legal claim to a right which is established by that rule.

A fundamental hypothesis involves the contention that a legal claim influences the legal position (i.e., rights and obligations) of other States. Essentially, this is undeniable since a legal claim can only apply to another subject or subjects. This claim is by definition directed *erga omnes*. This hypothesis is also undeniable if consideration is given to the reference of a legal right to which the claim refers, since legal rights do not exist in a vacuum but within a social sphere.

It is self-evident that although the claim is made *erga omnes*, some States may be more impacted than others, while the legal position of other States may remain unaffected. How can it be ascertained which State is affected by a specific legal claim? Two interrelated factors can add some clarity: the subject matter and the category of the action, especially whether the act is definite or indefinite in form.[4]

The Development of Legal Relationships

When a State performs a single act or a series of acts which support its legal claim, the response of other States is either positive or negative and may influence its legality. This could include whether the State will conform to the claim or oppose it. Opposability entails the capability of a legal rule or act producing an international effect vis-à-vis a State. It is from the standpoint of opposability that a legal relationship evolves; in short, the opposability of a claim facilitates the development of legal relationships.

Opposability of a legal claim is only applicable in a bilateral relationship. A central theme of all legal claims in the customary process is that they transmit a statement of willingness, by the claimant State, to have the same claim opposed against it, provided that the reacting State validates its claim.[5] An agreement to the reciprocal application of the legal claim can be explicit or implicit, and the claimant State may add certain qualifying conditions upon this commitment.

One such condition could involve strict conformity of the reacting State's claim with its own legal claim. A very good example of this is the Truman Proclamation with Respect to Coastal Fisheries in Certain Areas of the High Seas. This Proclamation notes that "the right of any State to establish conservation zones off its shores *in accordance with the above principles is conceded, provided that corresponding recognition* is given to any fishing interest of nationals of the United States which may exist in such areas."[6] Thus, once a situation of opposability is created, reciprocity is the definite principle that ensures that legal rights and duties are applied in a bilateral relationship.

It must be acknowledged that a legal claim may be *prima facie* contrary to general international law and still be opposable to a specific State. This justification could be supported by the premise that a significant part of customary international law falls under the purview of *jus dispositivium* (a law or rule capable of being modified by contrary consensual engagement), and in that condition, those rules may be derogated from *inter partes* (between parties). If this is not acknowledged, it would be very hard to explain the development of a customary process and how States can oppose an established customary international rule.

When does opposability come into play between two States? Opposability may become an issue in two instances:

1. Recognition of the competing claim by the reacting State; and
2. When a reacting State renunciates its own right when or if the right contradicts the claim by the first State.

Recognition as a concept means acknowledging a given legal claim by a State, and the results created by that claim are opposable and valid against the claim. Acknowledgement of this claim may be implied or explicit. When it comes to renunciation, recognition, and acquiescence represent similar meaning. Renunciation simply underscores the conduct by which a State renounces its rights, regardless of the formal context in which it was made. Renunciation suggests that the legal claim entails an issue that, in the opinion of the reacting State, is already regulated by international law in a manner inconsistent with the claim. Thus, a situation of opposability serves two purposes: the reacting State recognizing the legal claim and the reacting State abandoning its perceived right.

Negative Acts, Recognition, and Renunciation

As mentioned earlier, negative acts represent acts of legally relevant omissions. An omission may be legally irrelevant when a State does not act because it had no real knowledge of the act performed by the other State due to insufficient publicity or because the act has no legal bearing on the abstaining State. In these situations, an omission cannot be considered as an act that facilitates the creation of a legal relationship. With this in mind, it is highly likely that the assertion by the claimant State that a legal relationship exists would be challenged.

Opposability may help establish a legal relationship when a State fails to react to another State's legal claims with the goal of affecting its own legal interests. Within this context, the affected State has an obligation to react to the legal claims, and failure to do so may justify that abstention as a legally relevant act or behavior.

Omission of this kind may suggest acquiescence or implicit recognition on the part of the affected State. In essence, it may indicate that the affected State has agreed to or recognized the right claimed by the other State and the situation creates the legal claim.[7] Additionally, when this kind of omission occurs, the renunciation of the affected State's right may also be implicit; the affected State is then considered to have lost the right to rely upon its own rights or simply waive its rights *vis-à-vis* the claimant.[8]

One could challenge this by stating that the renunciation of a right cannot be presumed. However, asserting this suggests that this principle is only confined to cases where there are doubts over renunciation as a right. If recognition of or agreeing to a right claimed by another State is verified, and the claimed right is incompatible with the right held by the State that recognizes the claim, then the renunciation of the latter's right can be taken for granted. In these situations, when a State renounces its right, it also renounces its right to contest the legal claim it recognized.

A relevant omission occurs when an affected State refuses or fails to assert a protest against the act performed by the claimant State or reserves the right to do so in accordance with international law. The *Fisheries* case is a good example of this. In this case, the Court ruled that the Norwegian system of delimitation was opposable to the United Kingdom, noting that "the notoriety of the facts... Great Britain's position in the North Sea, her own interests in the question, and her prolonged abstention would in any case warrant Norway's enforcement of her system against the United Kingdom."[9]

When it comes to the development of a legal relationship, it does not really matter whether there is a lack of protest of the affected State. If an affected State does not render a protest within a specific time period, a legal claim and the act which it embodies could bring about a de facto situation between the two States, which would obviate the affected State from opposing the other State's legal claim in the future.[10]

So, if an affected State maintained a certain level of protest that did not recognize a legal claim, it could find itself in a situation where this protest is *prima facie* ineffective. In the *Land, Island, and Maritime Frontier Dispute* case, the Court maintained that a protest made by Honduras came "after a long history of acts of sovereignty by El Salvador in Meanguera, was made too late to affect the presumption of acquiescence on the part of Honduras."[11] The Court further stated that "the conduct of Honduras vis-à-vis earlier effectivities reveals an admission, recognition, acquiescence or other forms of tacit consent to the situation."[12]

A later denial by the affected State that it never intended to recognize or agree to the other State's legal claim may be true, but because of the situation that took place during the initial abstinence, the affected State is precluded from challenging the validity of the legal relationship that was created.[13] This is all the more true if the claimant State can prove that its conduct was clear and consistent and relied on (to its detriment) the conduct of the affected State and the situation it created.[14] In order to maintain peace and security within the global sphere, a State is not to assert a claim which is contrary to its past behavior.[15]

Hersch Lauterpacht has expanded on this issue. He suggests that the legal effects of the failure to lodge a protest in a timely manner may be justified on the account of the late protest being "an essential requirement of stability" and that it helps States from "incurring responsibilities and expense" by overly relying on the "acquiescence of others."[16]

Positive Acts, Recognition, and Renunciation

Positive acts represent another way that recognition and/or renunciation of legal claims are developed. Positive acts consist of solid and explicit instances of State practice. They facilitate the development of a legal relationship when they manifest recognition or assert/admission of a legal claim, or when they indicate that a reacting State has (by practice) adopted the same or similar legal claim.

Types of Recognition and Adoption

The difference between recognition and adoption of a legal claim can be shown in two ways:

1. Recognition without Adoption

When a reacting State supports the practice and the legal claim of another State without expressly adopting the same practice and claim. The 1971 issue that arose between Peru and China is a prime example. In this case, Peru and China issued a cooperative communique about the creation of diplomatic relations in which China recognized "the sovereignty of Peru over the maritime zone adjacent to her coasts within the limits of 200 nautical miles." This explicit support for Peru's claim was given by China, although China did not at the time adopt the same claim.[1]

This situation could lead to two outcomes:

1. There is a possibility that a State, in reacting to a legal claim by another State, recognizes or acknowledges the claim of a third State without adopting it. An excellent example is a diplomatic note sent by Japan in 1958 in response to a legal claim made by Mexico. In this communication, Japan recognized a claim asserted by the Scandinavian States, although it was not obligated to do so, which stated:

   > "it is, however, the view of the Government of Japan that the 3 miles breath for the territorial sea still remains to be a recognized rule under current international law and therefore, all claims for a broader breath may not be validly asserted, except the Scandinavian States' claims of 4 miles."[2]

2. In another instance, a State may also give an advance recognition of a specific legal claim, without specifying which State(s) to which the recognition is directed. It can even do this without adopting the legal

> claim itself. A prime example of this is the U.S. Presidential Statement that was amended to the Proclamation establishing a 200-mile Exclusive Economic Zone. This Statement asserted that "while international law provides for a right of jurisdiction over marine scientific research within such a zone, the Proclamation does not assert this right."[3] It further added that the United States would "recognize the right of other coastal States to exercise jurisdiction over marine scientific research within 200 nautical miles of their coasts, if that jurisdiction is exercise in a manner consistent with international law."[4]

This type of recognition, one that entails recognizing a claim which a State does not adopt itself, is generally granted by a State for the following reasons:

1. The State had no legal interest affected by the claim
2. It believes that it would be to its advantage to strengthen a legal claim
3. It believes it would likely adopt the claim in the future
4. It feels that the act would fulfill a political objective

2. Recognition with Adoption

When a reacting State both recognizes and adopts the legal claim.[5] Generally, States adopt claims through emulation. However, an emulated practice may not correspond completely with the practice of the claimant State. The reacting State may engage in a contradictory practice of its choosing, which may lead to a different legal claim. This can be the result when a reacting State follows a practice that involves a more extensive legal claim.

Consequently, in 1945 Chile implemented a Presidential decree concerning the Continental Shelf, which, despite highlighting the guidelines of the Truman Proclamation of 28 September 1945, was considered by the U.S. as breaching the terms of its own claims.[6]

The detailed protest of the American note stated:

> "At the same time, the United States Government notes that the principles underlying the Chilean Declaration differ in large measure from those of the United States Proclamation and appear to be at variance with the generally accepted principles of international law."[7]

In these types of instances, developing a legal relationship between the claimant and the reacting State may be weakened by the former's objection to the claim of the latter due to inherent differences. There is also the possibility that each legal claim may overlap.

Coordinated Recognition

Recognition itself may be formulated as a coordinated act. This act could be definite, indefinite, or both. There are many examples of coordinated acts when it comes to recognition.

The Governments of Chile, Ecuador, and Peru, in 1952, issued a Joint Declaration which they proclaimed as a "principle of their international maritime policy" that "each of them possesses sole sovereignty and jurisdiction over the area of the sea adjacent to the coast of its own country and extending no less than 200 nautical miles from said coast."[8] This act was definite because it secured the recognition of each other's claim – the declaration was directed toward one another – while it was also indefinite because it was implemented to present a common claim before the other States that were not a party to the agreement.

In a similar fashion, Colombia and Ecuador signed an agreement which "recognize and respect the procedures used by each State at present, and those that may be used in the future, for exercising its sovereignty, jurisdiction or supervision in those marine and submarine areas which are adjacent to its coast as far as 200 miles..."[9]

Impediments to Legal Relationships

On the other hand, some positive acts may impede the establishment of a legal relationship. One of the ways that a State may prevent a legal relationship is through diplomatic channels. A diplomatic protest may be asserted with a view to:

1. Manifesting the legal opinion of the State regarding the legal specifics of another State's legal claim
2. Expressing a reservation of its own rights as they pertain to the effects of the claims
3. Not recognizing a claim
4. Denying or not acknowledging any legal effects of the claim
5. Preventing the development of a new legal relationship between itself and the claimant State

In essence, the main purpose of a protest is to rebut the presumption of recognition, acquiescence or renunciation. Numbers (4) and (5) generally are the result of (1), (2), and (3).

For example, Syria, in 1981, implemented a law by which the breadth of its territorial sea was extended to 35 miles. Responding to this enactment, Israel sent a diplomatic note which stated:

In the view of the Government of Israel, there is no foundation in existing international law for Syria's claims (1) to extend the territorial sea to a breadth of thirty-five miles from the baselines from which the breadth of the territorial sea is measured and, accordingly, it does not recognize (3) the said Syrian measure, and reserves its rights and the rights of its nationals in respect of it (2).[10]

Requirements for Diplomatic Protests

The intended effect of any diplomatic protest involves the circumstances and reasons why the protest was issued. Both of these forms of diplomatic protests are qualified. Therefore, diplomatic protests have to go through the avenues of diplomatic communication and the State representative, that is, the competent authority working on behalf of the State. The protests must be:

1. Clear
2. Address the issue precisely
3. Be asserted within a reasonable time period after the legal claim has been put forth

The content of the protest is very important. Depending on the way that the protest is expressed, it can produce unwanted and/or unintended results. Therefore, in the *Land, Island and Maritime Frontier Dispute* case, the Chamber acknowledged that a protest made by El Salvador pertaining to the sale of an island by Honduras was related solely to that act, and that the protest only indicated a recognition of Honduras' claim implied by that act to sovereignty over the island in question.[11]

Effectiveness of Diplomatic Protests

Even if all guidelines are followed, it is still questionable whether a diplomatic protest will entail the intended legal effects. The question remains: will a single diplomatic protest be sufficient to result in a legal effect, or should the protests be a part of a cooperative effort of other States?

An argument could be made that a given legal claim creates a *continuous situation*, and the reaction of an affected State should persist until the situation reverts to the *status quo ante*.[12] In essence, a single diplomatic protest that is asserted in a timely manner and follows all guidelines for submitting a protest may still be insufficient to affect a legal claim.

If the affected State asserts a general protest against a legal claim, the State's assertion may be considered a legal relationship in terms of opposability. However, it may not impede the assertion of the claim nor the existence of current conditions between the parties. The *Minquiers and Ecrehos* case is a prime example of this. In this case, Judge Levi Carneiro noted that the "mere periodical and ineffectual paper protests" presented by France were insufficient to maintain its claim.[13] He added that while the British Government "acted and continued to exercise its sovereignty, the French Government was satisfied to make a *paper* protest."[14] The Judge further stated that the French government could have sought additional avenues to resolve the issue, such as through arbitration.[15]

Countermeasures Beyond Protests

As mentioned earlier, States that assert a legal claim generally act as if the right to the claim actually exists, and it is applicable and enforceable against other States. To address this situation, the affected State could apply additional counter-measures, such as retaliation and challenges to the legal claim. These responses by a State could be considered *actes concluants* – or conclusive acts – which characterize another form of protest.

Whether the actions taken by the affected State will compel the claimant State to withdraw its claim is debatable, since it depends on the latter's reaction. Examining State practice on claims involving maritime jurisdiction reveals that non-industrialized and less powerful States were prepared to enforce their legal claims against most of the industrialized, powerful States.[16] However, powerful States had recourse through bilateral instruments that allowed them to continue their operations in the area claimed by the State in question.[17]

Nevertheless, the fact that in many of these instruments the legal position of each party was explicitly reserved and the legal claim in question continued to be applicable not only against the opposing State but also against other States. In other words, the legal claim could be considered *de facto* effective.

Compromises and Their Effects

The compromise between the claimant State and the protesting State under the guise of a bilateral instrument resulted in a decrease in challenges and retaliation on the part of the protesting State, which enhanced the effectiveness of the legal claim. However, there is more to consider. The impact of the claim upon the customary process in the face of stiff opposition from powerful States encourages other less powerful States to pursue the same path.

For example, in the early seventies the decision-making process that influenced Brazil to claim a 200-mile territorial sea – an influential report developed by the Ministry of External Relations and the Navy – stated that the political and diplomatic costs of the measure that would be adopted is acceptable and that "those Latin American countries which have adopted a 200-mile claim have survived the protests and the sanctions."[18]

Another difficulty of protest that should be acknowledged is provided by the operation of intertemporal law. A legal claim that is maintained over an extensive period, even during periods of generalized protests, may facilitate unique legal claims that originated from new legal developments. For instance, the claim of sovereignty over the Falkland/Malvinas Islands by the United Kingdom was accompanied by a claim of the islanders' right to self-determination.[19] Essentially, even though Argentina maintained a general protest, it was confronted with a new legal issue that amended the original question. That question is the relationship between sovereignty and the right to self-determination.

When and if a reacting State adopts another State's legal claims, its status would be that of a claimant State, and it will generate a reaction from States affected by the new claim. This domino effect will either end up in a general practice or be challenged by opposing States. In conclusion, before a customary rule becomes established, an international practice on a particular issue may well reveal the existence of bilateral relationships created on the basis of opposability.

Effects of the General State of the Law

A legal claim is often asserted on an issue that some States (who are affected by the claim) believe is already regulated by international law. Of course, the State that makes a legal claim may assert that international law does not govern the issue or does not regulate it sufficiently because of changing circumstances. For instance, the Truman Proclamation on Coastal Fisheries notes, in its Preamble, that the Government of the United States views with concern "the inadequacy of present arrangements for the protection and perpetuation of the fisheries resources contiguous to its coasts."[1] However, under such circumstances, the legality of the claim as it pertains to existing law would be a matter under consideration. Whether the legality of the claim will be justified or upheld depends on the response of other States.

By their behavior or acts, the reacting States will either oppose the legal claim or support it. If they support or endorse the claim, then the claim will be considered valid and will progressively become general law. But if the reacting States oppose the legality of the claim, they will bring about changes in the general law due to their attitude. There are two seminal effects that may occur when a legal claim is opposed:

1. The opposition serves as a reinforcement of an established customary rule
2. The opposition not only fortifies the established customary rule but also refines and further defines the rule

Effect (2) takes place when States, in opposition to a legal claim on the grounds of illegality, define the prevailing customary rule from their perspective. Additionally, while resolving the conflict, a third party (generally a law-determining entity) is asked to define what the law is and whether the legal claim corresponds to or is consistent with it. In this situation, the rule is further developed by the definition given by the entity and the influence of the entity's decision on the State's perspective on the rule.

Under circumstances where both the claimant State and the reacting State agree that there is no settled law on the issue, their acts will contribute to the definition of what the law is. In essence, the act accomplished by a State to support its legal claim, coupled with the reaction of other States to the claim, determines whether the law on the issue subsists as it was before the claim or will ultimately be changed or superseded.

International Organizations

International organizations, and their outlying entities and procedures, influence the development of the customary process in many ways. The various ways that this happens are analyzed below.

Identification and Definition of Customary Rules

Some organs of international organizations have taken on the role of law-determining agencies, determining the existence and extent of the contents that comprise established customary rules. A good example of this is the International Court of Justice, an auxiliary of the United Nations (UN Charter, Chapter XIV). The ICJ has, on various occasions, certified some customary rules whose existence and/or content were in dispute by contending States. In the *Continental Shelf Case (Libya v. Malta)*, the Court reasoned that "the institution of the exclusive economic zone, with its rule on entitlement by reason of distance, is shown by the practice of States to have been a part of customary law."[2] The Court also highlighted customary rules pertaining to non-intervention, non-use of force, collective self-defense, diplomatic relations, and maritime delimitation.[3]

This vast law-determining role emphasizes the authority of the ICJ assigned to it by its Statute. This function gives the ICJ the empowerment "to decide in accordance with international law such disputes as are submitted to it" (Art. 38). In resolving a dispute, it must first ascertain what the relevant law is. It should be noted that the Court, in giving its opinion of a customary rule, is also describing the state of the respective customary process to see whether the process is in the developmental process, has matured, or if the law(s) are in a state of certainty or uncertainty.

Although the Court's decision "has no binding force except between the parties and in respect of that particular case,"[4] this does not diminish its law-determining role. There can be a distinction made between the ascertainment of the general state of the law on a specific issue and the application of that law to a particular case. While the decision of the ICJ cannot bind third parties, it can determine the general state of law which transcends the limited scope *ratione personae* of the decision. This suggests that the decision can influence the legal perception of other States. This is the main reason why the Statute also refers, through Article 38(d), to judicial decisions "as subsidiary means for the determination of rules of law." One leading expert notes that this provision refers to the decision of the Court itself.[5]

The International Law Commission is another United Nations auxiliary that is empowered to perform a law-identifying role. The ILC is tasked with promoting the codification and progressive evolution of international law. One of its central functions involves investigating some of the content of customary rules. In fact, when ascertaining the outcome of a specific issue, which in most cases comes under the auspices of a Draft Convention, the ILC sometimes explicitly notes that a given article reflects international customary law. Consequently, in the Draft Articles on the Law of Treaties, the ILC, commenting on the proposed Article 59 (which references *rebus sic stantibus*), noted that "the evidence of the principle in customary law is considerable."[6]

The Security Council is a UN entity that is basically a political organ. However, it is charged with ascertaining or defining legal terms during certain international disputes and other contentious issues. Although in certain cases it abstains from referencing a specific rule, the legal definition it makes of a given situation reveals the underlying rule as standard international law. A good illustration is the East Timor question that arose in 1975. In that year, the Security Council implemented a resolution which denounced the "intervention of the armed forces of Indonesia in East Timor" and requested that all States "respect the territorial integrity of East Timor" along with "the inalienable right of its people to self-determination in accordance with General Assembly resolution 1514 (XV)."[7] Regarding this decision, three rules were the defining factor:

1. The rule that pertains to non-intervention
2. The rule of self-determination
3. The rule that relates to territorial integrity

During the international crisis that arose when Iraq occupied Kuwait, the Security Council made determinations based on the issues of sovereignty, independence and territorial integrity, and humanitarian law.[8] In these decisions, the SC was explicitly applying the rules embodied in the UN Charter rather than relevant rules of customary international law. If the premise is accepted that the conventional rules of the UN Charter facilitate the development of customary rules, then the activity of the SC may contribute to the definition and development of customary international law. In this case, the ICJ seems to support this proposition when it noted:

> "So far from having constituted a marked departure from a customary international law still unmodified, the Charter gave expression in this field to principles already present in customary international law, and that law has in subsequent decades developed under the influence of the Charter, to such an extent that a number of rules contained in the Charter have acquired a status independent of it."[9]

Nevertheless, the SC did not seem to have depended solely on the UN Charter provisions. In a corresponding Resolution, the SC referred to Iraq's flagrant violation of international humanitarian law.[10]

In addition to these UN auxiliaries, there are other organs within the UN structure that also express their views regarding customary international law. The United Nations Secretariat has performed this role on various occasions. In one of its legal decisions, it proclaimed that the provisions of the 1969 Vienna Convention on the Law of Treaties "are regarded as restating the customary international law of treaties," which includes "article 11 of the Convention."[11]

Regional organizations also have a definitive role in ascertaining law-determining activities. The Inter-American Juridical Committee is one such organization. It has the power to promote the codification and progressive development of international law.[12] Since the early 1900s, this organization has made many decisions regarding the state of customary international law. In the mid-1960s, for example, the IAJC implemented a resolution which stated that the "principles and rules that faithfully reflect the existing customary rule of international law" mirror "the right of every American State to fix the breadth of its territorial sea up to a limit of twelve nautical miles measured from the applicable base line."[13]

Whether or not the decisions of these UN organs make a positive impact upon customary international law is both subjective and debatable. The assessment of their decisions must be made from a broader framework. As mentioned earlier, the international system is anarchic, and because of this fact, the customary process is decentralized. While this may be an immutable fact of the international system, individual States may still influence the customary process through the aggregation of their practices. While this may impact the evolution of a customary rule, it does not define when a customary rule has matured.

Organs which determine the law, such as those examined above, not only influence how States perceive the existence of a mature customary rule, but also help determine the definition of the rule's content. The general content of a rule may be further interpreted when the rule is applied to a specific case germane to the organ in question. This law-defining mechanism is important to the customary process. Considering the mutable nature of the international system, States may interpret international rules and principles subjectively. This discretionary interpretation, which generally results in different perspectives of the rules, applies to both the content of the rule at hand and to the applicability of the rule to a specific issue. A very good example of this is the *Gulf of Maine* case. In this case, the Chamber reasoned that both parties agreed over the fundamental norm to be applied, although there was a dispute as to how it applied to the case in question.[14] If States' views differ on the content or how the customary rule will be applied, it is probable that their practice will also be different. Thus, the organs mentioned above help to ensure that the customary process runs smoothly by resolving the unpredictability associated with customary international law.

While law-determining organs may stress that their findings correlate with current State practice, the fact remains that their declarations often exert influence upon States. At the very minimum, these declarations strengthen international law by confirming it. If the customary process was considered a bargaining process, law-determining reasoning that comes from these organs would either help define the issue or end the debate surrounding the issue or strengthen the position of the actors who hold a similar view. For instance, in the *Rainbow Warrior* case, the Arbitral Tribunal relied on the International Law Commission's draft on State Responsibility as an indication of the customary law on the issue.[15] Of course, the extent to which the findings influence the State's actions and perception of the law will differ according to the organ in question. Even two decisions coming from the same organ may have two entirely different results.

Based on the analysis above, there is a thin line separating the organ's law-determining role and law-creating role. The Court's activities seem to support this premise. An initial reading of the Court's Statute would generally lead one to assume that the Court has no competence to engage in judicial activism. Unless the parties involved in the dispute agree to a decision *ex aequo et bono*, the Court is only required to apply existing international law to the dispute. Yet, owing to the mutable nature of customary international law, the guidelines of generality and uniformity in the practice, not to mention the difficult task of ascertaining the exact moment in which a custom has matured, the decisions of the Court in contentious cases can be labeled as little more than legislation, or as judicial inspiration.[16] Acknowledging these difficulties, one leading scholar noted that:

> "In few matters do judicial discretion and freedom of judicial appreciation manifest themselves more conspicuously than in determining the existence of international custom... many an act of judicial legislation may in fact be accomplished under the guise of the ascertainment of customary international law."[17]

For example, in the *Gulf of Maine* case, the Chamber stated that the Court's Judgment in the *North Sea Continental Shelf* cases had made "the greatest contribution" to the development of international law in this area.[18]

Besides the law ascertaining capabilities mentioned above, international organizations determine laws in other ways. They provide a platform where legal positions and justifications for the State's actions are demonstrated. Members of the UN send legal protests, reservations, and justifications concerning a particular State practice or issue to the Secretary-General or the President of the Security Council via diplomatic Notes. This procedure allows States to send messages that will reach the largest possible degree of publicity and compels competent organs to express their views on the legality of another State's behavior. This also permits communications between States that do not maintain formal diplomatic relations. In the South West Africa case, Judge Tanaka noted that:

> "A State, instead of pronouncing its view to a few States directly concerned, has the opportunity, through the medium of an organization, to declare its position to all members of the organization and to know immediately their reaction on the same matter."[19]

Such procedures are very important because they help determine the validity of the law by allowing other States to evaluate pertinent evidence that relates to the issue at hand. A legal view asserted by a State, pertaining to a legal claim or specific behavior, could have been the result of adjusting the relevant law to its own political objectives. Diplomatic Notes and communications sent to the Secretary-General may contain vital information about the law, which can give clarity to a particular situation. For example, the United States, in 1987, sent a communication to the UN Secretary-General in which it opposed a claim made by Viet Nam and the People's Republic of Kampuchea to certain alleged historic waters in the Gulf of Thailand. In the communication, the US restated what it called "long-standing standards of customary international law and State practice" with respect to the requisites that have to be fulfilled in order that historic waters are acknowledged as valid. The text stated:

> "As is well known under long-standing standards of customary international law and State practice, historic waters are recognized as valid if the following prerequisites are satisfied: (A) the State asserting claims thereto has done so openly and notoriously; (B) the State has

effectively exercised its authority over a long and continuous period; and (C) other States have acquiesced therein."[20]

The Development of Customary Rules

Through their practices, International Organizations may participate in the customary process. Historical antecedents support this proposition.[21] The qualifying factor is that their direct participation is limited to those areas where they are acting in their own interests. Hence, reference could be made to the immunity of international organizations as allowed by international law. However, in many instances, IOs only take part in the customary process on an indirect basis. Still, the various ways in which international organizations influence the development of the customary process are a worthy subject to examine.

However, it is also a subject that is rife with controversy. While there have been in-depth (and at times contentious) debates about this issue, it is very difficult to dismiss the practice of certain international organizations in areas such as the law of treaties. Other international intergovernmental organizations are considered supranational organizations to which States have transferred some exclusive competences. The European Union is a prime example of this. These supranational entities exercise some of the powers allocated to States and thus, contribute to practice and *opinio juris.* The International Law Commission addresses this topic in a report entitled *Identification of Customary International Law.* Under this report, Draft Conclusion 4, paragraph 1 explicitly states that the central requirement for practice is that "it is *primarily*" a domain of States "that contributes to" the development of customary international law. Draft Conclusion 4, paragraph 2 notes that:

> "In certain cases, the practices of international organizations also contribute to the formation, or expression, of rules of customary international law."[22]

An addendum to this text states:

> "The Drafting committee provisionally adopted Draft Conclusion 4 with the understanding that this draft conclusion would be considered again at the next session in light of the analysis of the question of the practice of international organizations that will be part of the third report of the Special Rapporteur."[23]

However, is the practice and *opinio juris* of subjects of international law other than states and international organizations relevant? This question seems to have escaped the attention of the Drafting Committee. Questions may come into focus regarding sui generis organs, such as the International Committee of the Red Cross. Non-governmental organizations and other private organizations would seem to have no direct role. Although they may be influential, this influence is only the result of the reactions of States that may also influence the law.

In 2014, the discussion of this topic continued at the Sixth Committee of the United Nations General Assembly. The representative of the United States raised concern:

> "that the treatment of international organizations together with States in Draft conclusion 4 may be taken to suggest that these actors play the same roles with respect to the formation of custom, obscuring, in particular, significant limitations on the role of international organizations in this respect....

While we are not persuaded as yet that the practice of international organizations is of general relevance to the identification of custom, we are open to the possibility that there may be circumstances in which some activities of international organizations may contribute to the formation of customary international law."[24]

If we accept the premise that international organizations may contribute to the formation of customary international law, then some very difficult questions would have to be addressed.

In the first instance, the practice and *opinio juris* of those international organizations to which member States have transferred exclusive competences would fall within the purview of a unique category. Their practice may be on the same level as other member States, especially when organizations serve as a proxy for member States. This involves actions of such organizations, whether these actions are executive, legislative, or judicial in nature. If the practice of international organizations was not on the same level as states, not only would the organization's practice not contribute to a general practice, but its member States would be deprived of their ability to contribute to such practice in cases where they have transferred power to the organization.

The second question to consider is: which entities of international organizations are relevant to the customary process? Such entities may be divided as:

1. Entities composed of States (i.e., the United Nations General Assembly)
2. Secretariats, who play an important political role (i.e., UN Secretary-General)
3. Entities that consist of individuals that are appointed for definitive purposes (i.e., the Special Rapporteur for human rights appointed by the Human Rights Council)

With all things considered, there is support for the notion that the practice and *opinio juris* of entities to which member States have transferred power is most important when it comes to contributing to a general practice. As concisely expressed by a member of the Commission, the main difference lies between the products of the secretariats of international organizations and those of the intergovernmental organs of international organizations. While both can provide pertinent information that can be consulted, the "greater relative weight... [is to be] given to the products of the latter, whose authors were also the primary authors of State practice."[25] However, the actions of secretariats may also be important. For instance, the exercise of treaty depositary functions of the United Nations and other secretariats. On the contrary, the practice of organs that are comprised of individuals serving in their personal capacity cannot be considered as an official representation of States nor the organization.

Thirdly, in ascertaining the practice of international organizations, there needs to be a distinction made between practice relating to the domestic affairs of the organization and the practice of the organization as it pertains to States and international organizations. But the dividing line may not be easy to discern.

Fourth, is it required for the organization to act within its inherent powers and functions for its acts to count? Maybe, but it is not clear why acts that are *ultra vires* – acts performed outside legal or authority parameters – should not also count. It is difficult to assess whether or not an organization is acting *ultra vires* in a given situation. There is usually no centralized authority to make such a judgment.

In the fifth instance, can inaction by an international organization play a definitive role when it comes to determining customary international rules? Inaction, or acquiescence, of States plays an important part in the development of customary international rules.

Finally, which rules of international law may the practice and *opinio juris* of organs of international organizations be applied to help determine what is international law and what is not? It is generally considered that the rules that bind States are those that primarily contribute to the development of international law. The final point highlights another important issue: to what extent are international organizations bound by the rules of customary international law? That they are bound is very clear.[26] However, there seems to be very little discussion of the extent of international obligations as they pertain to international organizations. In some instances, it is asserted that organizations have an international personality and thus have certain international rights and obligations which bind them under international law.[27] Yet, this may not entirely be the case.

Jose Alvarez, in his work on *International Organizations as Law-Makers,* noted that:

> "It... remains uncertain whether organizations... are liable for violations of customary law, especially since it is not clear whether the rules of custom, such as the rules arising under international humanitarian law, apply in exactly the same way to IOs."[28]

Dapo Akande makes a valid point when he stated that:

> "[P]ossessing international legal personality means that an organization possesses rights and duties in international law, but this does not usually tell us the particular rights and capacities possessed by a particular organization."[29]

This leads to the question: What is the exact position? As the Commission acknowledged in its General Commentary to its draft articles on the *Responsibility of International Organizations,* "International organizations are quite different from States, and in addition present great diversity among themselves. There are very significant differences among international organizations with regard to... the primary rules including treaty obligations by which they are bound."[30] While the comments regarding treaty obligations are obvious, most international organizations are not parties to treaties. With this in mind, the position regarding customary international law, as expressed by the Commission, remains much more complex.[31]

The Codification and Development of International Law

The United Nations' international legislative efforts provide an excellent illustration of methods for creating and developing general international law. The UN has employed various procedures aimed at developing multilateral conventions that fulfill the General Assembly's Charter-mandated function: the codification and gradual development of international law. Rules contained within these resulting conventions are inviolable and often reflect existing customary international law, sometimes representing such customary law even before the conventions formally enter into force. To properly understand the role of codifying conferences and conventions, one must view them within the broader context of general international law development.

The Importance of Law-Making Procedures

The UN Secretary-General examined the methods used to promote and facilitate multilateral treaty-making activities in a Report prepared for the thirty-fifth session of the General Assembly.[1] Several key points emerge from this report:

First, procedures are implemented to ensure States can participate in all three main stages of the multilateral treaty development process:

1. The formative stages of the draft
2. Commentary and debates pertaining to the draft
3. Discussion and negotiation rounds
4. Formal adoption during the closing stages of the conference

When procedures involve the International Law Commission (ILC) as the drafting entity, States may play an even more definitive role. According to the ILC's Statute, States must be given opportunities to maintain direct relationships with the ILC's work at each stage. This occurs when States are required to supply information and pertinent data concerning items in the ILC's action plan, or when the General Assembly requests State comments on specific draft items submitted to the ILC. States may also express their perspectives on ILC drafts through the Sixth Committee and the General Assembly.[2] Following in-depth discussions and negotiations, draft proposals can be adopted in ways that reflect the legal positions of the States. This demonstrates the importance of unratified conventions as they relate to existing customary international law or to the development of such law.

Despite efforts by the International Law Commission, some resulting agreements remain unratified and unlikely to enter into force. This highlights certain shortcomings in law-making procedures and raises questions about whether such agreements represent a complete picture of customary international law's general nature. However, this does not render law-making procedures irrelevant—rather, it indicates that in specific cases, procedures were either inappropriate or improperly applied. Ian Sinclair commented on why some agreements succeed while others fail, noting that "the process itself is more important" than the mechanism or content used to achieve codification.[3]

Another important factor concerns the preparatory work and procedural efforts adopted by the UN. In certain cases, this preparatory work is conducted either by the ILC itself or by *ad hoc* or proxy bodies specifically designed for this purpose. The composition of the ILC and other auxiliary entities tends to reflect not only important global legal systems but also crucial interests that must be addressed. This has been accomplished by apportioning available seats according to geographical regions (as with the ILC) or by composing entities with members from States having an interest in the issues. As Roberto Ago explained, this procedure ensures that perspectives and interests likely to arise at codifying conferences are already represented within drafting bodies.[4] Consequently, potential difficulties regarding the drafting or acceptance of provisions can be addressed early, improving chances for success at subsequent conferences.

Additionally, procedures implemented within the UN typically provide follow-up mechanisms to help with verification, ratification, compliance, and implementation of adopted provisions. These "checks and balances" may take various forms:

1. Entities to which States must report periodically or upon request
2. Actions encouraging compliance and ratification
3. Collateral activities such as information dissemination about conventions and their status
4. Provision of international technical assistance when required[5]

These mechanisms represent legal and political forces inducing States to conform to rules embodied within agreements. Therefore, procedures implemented by entities indirectly contribute to the development of international practice.

Codifying Conferences and Conventions

The UN's primary legislative work centers on convening multilateral conferences for the codification and progressive development of customary international law. Since the International Court of Justice's ruling in the *North Sea Continental Shelf* cases, doctrine has supported the notion that codifying agreements may produce three direct effects upon customary processes:

1. Proclaiming existing law
2. Solidifying customary practice into custom
3. Generating new custom[6]

The customary process related to the Exclusive Economic Zone provides an excellent case study supporting this proposition. Examining international practice and its relationship to the EEZ concept clarifies the role that the EEZ plays in forming customary international law.

Chapter VII
The Development of Customary International Law and the Two-Hundred-Mile EEZ

The precise relationship between state practice and the formation of customary international law has been a highly debated issue among various commentators. Authors and legal experts disagree on the relative importance of the particular elements needed to forge the relationship between state practice and customary international law, and debates also surround the specific elements regarding this relationship.[1] However, Manley O. Hudson,[2] along with the decisions rendered by the ICJ, has identified the rubrics of customary international law as:

a. widespread and consistent state practice;[3]

b. repetition of the practice over a considerable time period;[4]

c. the practice performed out of a sense of obligation;[5] and

d. the practice must be taken by a significant number of states and not rejected by a significant number of states.[6]

Widespread and Consistent State Practice

In the *North Sea Continental Shelf Cases*, the ICJ insisted on "a very widespread and representative participation ... state practice, including that of states whose interests are especially affected, should have been extensive and virtually uniform."[7] Judge Lachs, in a dissenting statement, gave clarity to the terms widespread and representative, and noted that "states with different political, economic, and legal systems, states of all continents should participate in this process."[8] Judge D'Arechaga, giving a separate opinion in the *Continental Shelf (Tunisia v. Libya) Case* noted that "the proclamation by 86 coastal states of economic zones, fishery zones, or fishery conservation zones ... constitutes a widespread practice of states."[9]

According to one leading commentator, "the practice must be general not universal... the practice must have been applied by the overwhelming majority of states which hitherto has an opportunity of applying it."[10] Corbett noted that there has to be a sense of "general approval"[11] among the states, whereas Tunkin believes that general practice itself does not necessarily mean the practice of all states.[12] The ICJ supported the notion that universality is not a key requirement.[13]

The most important element is uniformity and consistency.[14] In this context, the ICJ said in the *Asylum Case* that "the Colombian Government must prove that the rule invoked by it is in accordance with a constant and uniform usage practice by the states in question."[15] Lauterpacht echoed this sentiment by stating there should be "concordant international practice."[16] The central point is that there should not be much "uncertainty and contradiction, so much fluctuation and discrepancy" in state practice.[17] Minor inconsistency in state practice does not prevent the creation of a customary rule. In this context, the ICJ, in the *Nicaragua v. United States Case*,[18] emphasized that the practice in question did not have to be "in absolute rigorous conformity" with the purported customary rule. The Court further stated that:

"In order to deduce the existence of customary rules, the Court deems it sufficient that the conduct of states should, in general, be consistent with such rules, and that instances of state conduct inconsistent with a given rule should generally have been treated as breaches of that rule, not as indications of the recognition of a new rule."[19]

As mentioned in Chapter Four, during the time period between 1975 and 1978, over forty coastal states established their own two-hundred-mile jurisdictional zones that related to fisheries and certain other issues such as MSR and the preservation of the marine environment.[20] An additional sixteen EEZ claims were made between 1978 and 1981.[21] This same time period also saw other coastal states establish their own two-hundred-mile EFZ rather than establishing a full EEZ.[22]

It must be remembered that legal scholars who have argued against the binding nature of the EEZ under the general principles of customary international law have mainly relied on two central arguments:

1. The partial and provisional nature of certain two-hundred-mile EEZ claims;
2. The complete "package deal" analogy that ruled out any selective application of the provisions of the LOS Convention.

For the first argument, some asserted that some coastal states have implemented claims to a two-hundred-mile EFZ only when these claims promoted a provisional element of the state's practice, which ultimately resulted in the non-uniformity of the jurisdictional zone. In this context, one legal scholar stated:

> "If we ... look at state practice and we try to analyze the acts adopted by governments, we must come to the conclusion that all of them differ

greatly. For example, if we look at the act of the USSR, adopted in 1976, we note that this act will be in force until the date of the entry into force of the convention, and that it said nothing about establishing the exclusive economic zone. So, if we analyze all the acts adopted by different states, we find that there is no reason to say that we have a generally recognized practice. For this reason, we cannot say that the exclusive economic zone is a norm of customary law."[23]

But this argument can be countered by simply acknowledging that the fishery regime is a vital element of the EEZ concept and that the exploitation and conservation of fisheries resources located in adjacent seas has been the central basis for the establishment of the two-hundred-mile EEZ since the 1940s. In essence, any claim based primarily on the exclusive fishery zone strengthens the concept of the EEZ.[24]

In addition, it is reasonable to add to the argument of gradual implementation of the EEZ concept into state practice as evidenced, for example, by the approach coastal states take to proclaim exclusive fishery zones. In the far sight, the EEZ may well replace all exclusive fishery zones. This appears to be confirmed by the transformation of an existing two-hundred-mile EFZ into an EEZ, which was implemented by the United States in 1983,[25] the Soviet Union in 1984,[26] Poland in 1991,[27] Sweden in 1993,[28] and Australia in 1994.[29]

The Package Deal Argument

Regarding the package deal dynamics, certain states, such as the former Soviet Union,[30] argued that UNCLOS III resolved all the issues of the sea (under the regimes of the territorial sea, EEZ, international straits, the high seas, continental shelf, and the international seabed area), by combining these problems under one complete package, dramatically improving the effectiveness of the LOS Convention's rules and principles.[31] Thus, the result of this premise is that acceptance of the LOS Convention as a binding instrument that forms a package deal may be considered a source of customary international law only in its totality and not with respect to any selective element of its provisions, such as the concept of the EEZ. Various commentators have supported this argument, particularly following the early years of the LOS Convention, as an essential argument against the global binding nature of the EEZ.[32]

Although the package deal seems to be a viable argument from the standpoint of legal debates and conventional norms, the argument itself is still questionable, mainly because it fails to appreciate the effective role that state practice has when it comes to establishing customary international law, which is a focal point of the formation of the basic principles of international law.[33] This could result in nullifying the legal force of customary international law by way of conventional exclusiveness, which in turn would destabilize international law itself.[34]

Eastern European, Western, and developing states do not subscribe to the package-deal argument, which emphasizes the nature of the EEZ.[35] In fact, most Western legal publicists consider the package deal something of a procedural mechanism designed specifically to further the achievement of consensus, as expressed by UNCLOS III, which has questionable merits at best.[36] Furthermore, they regard state practice as the primary test of whether third states may enjoy rights that are stipulated in treaties. In this connection, Lee observed:

> "Even if the intent of the negotiations of the law of the sea Convention was to limit the benefits of all its provisions to the signatories as parties to a so-called package deal, non-party states may enjoy the same benefits if the particular provision of the Convention ... has since acquired the status of customary rule through widespread acceptance as law and confirmation by state practice."[37]

Additionally, a chamber of the ICJ, in the *Gulf of Maine Case*, reasoned that:

> "The Chamber notes in the first place that the Convention ... has not yet come into force and that a number of states does not appear inclined to ratify it. This however, in no way detracts from the consensus reached on large portions of the instrument and, above all, cannot invalidate the observation that certain provisions of the Convention, concerning the... exclusive economic zone ... were adopted without any objections. ... In the Chamber's opinion, those provisions, even if in some respects they bear the mark of the compromise surrounding their adoption, may nevertheless be regarded as consonant at present with general international law on that question."[38]

Hence, considering the number of states that have implemented unilateral legislation creating EEZs and EFZs up to a breadth of two hundred miles, *prima facie* state practice is extensive and uniform.[39] Moreover, coastal states whose interests are severely affected generally have incorporated the formulation of the concept into the texts of their negotiating instruments.

Repetition of the Practice over a Considerable Time Period

Hans Kelsen, in his seminal work *Principles of International Law*, stated that "custom by which a norm of general international law is created" is a "long-established practice of states."[1] Brian Lepard seemed to concur with this assessment when he wrote that "widespread and contiguous state practice will usually be necessary evidence of" customary international law.[2] However, in some instances, this requirement is less stringent. In this connection, in the *North Sea Continental Shelf Cases*, the ICJ made a point that it is not necessary to prove that a specific practice had to be followed for a certain length of time.[3] Thus, the notion of a "long-established" practice is considered a chief requirement because it would negate the possibility of creating new customary norms, even when state actions are "uniform and universal" in practice.[4]

State practice concerning the two-hundred-mile EEZ has grown exorbitantly. This rapid growth prompted Shigeru Oda to comment that "throughout the history of international law, scarcely any other major concept has ever stood at the threshold of acceptance within such a short period."[5]

Opinio Juris

The requirement for the *opinio juris* element is referenced as the "psychological and recognition component" needed to create the formation of a custom.[6] In essence, the actions by the state correlate with internationally accepted principles of law.[7] Declarations, draft proposals, and official statements made at UNCLOS III are the main forum from which the *opinio juris* element evolved. During this Conference, particularly at the 1974 Caracas Session, virtually all the states supported the notion of a two-hundred-mile EEZ.[8] Other instances in which the *opinio juris* element can be inferred or identified include proclamations of national legislation, ratification of the LOS Convention, fishery and delimitation instruments regarding the two-hundred-mile EEZ, and legal opinions.[9] All these areas represent states' intent in recognizing the legal nature of their practices.

Rejection and Acceptance

Protest and acquiescence are key elements that need to be acknowledged when determining whether a practice is a customary norm.[10] These two elements are also important when determining whether a state practice is uniform and extensive.[11] Hence, when a pattern of state practice is emerging, some states may choose to stage a persistent objection to such practice, preventing it from becoming a general customary rule. A state's persistent objection is one way a state can protest a particular practice.[12] With this in mind, several judges in the Fisheries Jurisdiction Case noted that EFZs exceeding twelve miles did not create norms because of persistent objections from other states.[13]

But in some instances, states do nothing *vis-à-vis* a known practice but stay silent on the issue. In these cases, the issue that must be confronted is whether such a silence should indicate complete dissatisfaction with an emerging state practice, or does the silence indicate that the state agreed with the practice. The

ICJ was forced to consider a similar problem in *The Temple of Preah Vihear Case*. In this case, the Court reasoned that long-continued silence on the part of Thailand over a drawn boundary line prepared for Cambodia indicated that Thailand agreed with the drawn boundary line.[14] The Court stated that acquiescence can be assumed if there is "a failure to react ... on an occasion that called for a reaction in order to affirm or preserve [the claim] in the face of an obvious rival claim."[15]

Pertinent to the rapid growth of the EEZ concept, more than seventy states developed EEZs or EFZs between the years 1974 and 1981.[16] Protests were required from other interested states when Mexico first implemented a law based on the RSNT when the enforcement date was set for June 6, 1976,[17] only a month after the Fifth Session of UNCLOS III had ended in New York. Neither the GDS, LLS, nor major industrial states objected to the EEZ concept. In fact, the GDS and LLS sought to preserve some rights for themselves regarding this concept,[18] and the major maritime states were open to the concept, provided they could exercise non-economic rights in the zone.

Acceptance of a practice cannot be presumed unless a state has knowledge that a claim is being made. Regarding the circumstances involving Mexico, it does not seem plausible that participating states in the Fifth Session of UNCLOS III knew nothing about the claims that Mexico put forth. In fact, Mexico's action was followed by various other coastal states. In addition, during the early seventies, protests primarily came from the states of Japan, the United Kingdom, and West Germany. These states eventually developed their own two-hundred-mile EFZs. In essence, desistence from protest by these states, combined with the notion that these states eventually developed their own EFZ, suggests not only that these states modified their position, but also provides evidence that they were willing to accept new customary rules regarding the two-hundred-mile EFZ.

As the above analysis indicates, claims to the two-hundred-mile EEZ have satisfied the requirements set by international law for state practice regarding the establishment of customary norms. Thus, as noted in several judicial decisions rendered by the ICJ and arbitration panels[19] and expressed by various international legal experts,[20] the two-hundred-mile EEZ is an integral part of customary international law. As a result, the assertions made by Iguechi[21] and Zakharov,[22] as well as by other noted commentators concerning the nonbinding nature of the EEZ under the rubric of customary law, seem to be problematic.

The Scope of the EEZ Concept in Customary International Law

The importance of the analysis of the main components of the EEZ concept as it relates to customary international law is a central focus of a number of legal experts, especially those from Western Europe. The school of thought these legal experts support involves doubts as to whether the rights of coastal states other than those with an interest in the living resources are part of the customary law rule concerning the two-hundred-mile EEZ.[1] In this context, Fleischer stated, "In state practice, it is the right to 200 miles for fisheries which commands the largest measure of general international acceptance, while the right to a full EEZ under contemporary customary law may be more questionable."[2] Thus, under customary international law, the right to assert a two-hundred-mile zone for fisheries involves a more comprehensive view of the EEZ concept.

National Practice

Many key concepts expressed at UNCLOS III played a considerable role in the implementation of such national instruments as official proclamations, decrees, and legislative measures. These acts became a defining force in state practice. Hence, when EEZ national claims are closely analyzed, it is easy to see the significance of the EEZ concept expressed in Article 56 of the LOS Convention or some of the negotiating texts that led to the development of the Convention.

Germane to the assertion of sovereign rights in exploring and exploiting the living and non-living resources of the EEZ and regarding the direct and collateral economic activities pertaining to the EEZ expressed in Article 56(1)(a) of the LOS Convention, there exists a near-absolute consensus on the national level. Essentially, with the exception of a very few EEZ claims that fail to refer to sovereign rights regarding activities that pertain to other economic uses of the EEZ, all other EEZ claims mirror the general principles of coastal states' sovereign rights reflected in Article 56(1)(a).[3]

Furthermore, except for a small percentage of EFZ claims[4] and fewer EEZ claims, all other EEZ claims include a provision that pertains to coastal states' jurisdiction over artificial islands, installations, and structures, and also includes provisions relating to the marine environment. In this context, of the 87 claims to the EEZ, 57 states claimed jurisdiction over artificial islands, installations, and structures in the EEZ;[5] 63 of these states asserted jurisdiction over MSR;[6] and over 80 states claimed jurisdiction over environmental safety issues.7 Although these claims of jurisdiction vary according to the circumstances involved, variations do not represent a significant change in the basic components of the EEZ concept outlined in Article 56(1)(b) of the LOS Convention, mostly because they relate to the specific regimes governing the activities that pertain to the fundamental component of the EEZ concept. Moreover, the EEZ is a package-deal network that comprises the rights of coastal states, as well as their duties and rights and the duties of third states. The rights and duties of each of these groups of states correspond to the concept of the EEZ.

As mentioned earlier in Chapter four, a majority of EEZ claims have explicitly or implicitly acknowledged the basic rights contained in Article 58(1) of the LOS Convention, which belongs to third states and involves the freedom of navigation, overflight, and laying of submarine cables and pipelines. One legal expert highlighted the magnitude of national practice in this field by noting, "As a general rule, the freedom of navigation, overflight, and the laying of submarine cables and pipelines as well as other associated freedoms, are recognized at the conceptual level."[8]

Additionally, in its decision of June 10, 1992 in the Case Concerning the Delimitation of the Maritime Areas between Canada and the French Republic, the Arbitral Tribunal reasoned that "the principle of freedom of navigation through the 200-mile zone is guaranteed by Article 58 of the 1982 Convention, a provision that undoubtedly represents customary international law as much as the institution of the 200-mile zone itself."[9]

Recent Jurisprudence of the ICJ

Five decades have passed since the four Geneva Conventions on the LOS were implemented,[10] but their acceptance was not as widely accepted as UNCLOS III.[11] However, some states with major maritime interests are not signatories to one or more of these instruments.[12]

Over the past five decades, various international agreements have made formal reference to the relationship between customary international law and the LOS Convention.[13] This raises the issue of which provisions in these instruments are considered binding on all states under the principles of customary international law. A second and equally important question is which rules of customary international law that do not have a counterpart in LOS treaties are applicable to the principles of the LOS. The judicial decisions of the ICJ and other tribunals provide the answer to the first question. The answer to the second question can be found in the decisions and opinions of the International Tribunal for the Law of the Sea (ITLOS) and arbitration organizations.[14] Table 1 provides a comprehensive list of the cases in which the ICJ and other tribunals have addressed the relationship between customary international law and the provisions of UNCLOS III. Table 2 provides a list of the cases that have identified rules of customary norms that are not a part of LOS treaties, but are applicable in the context of the LOS.

Table VII.1: Cases Addressing Customary International Law and UNCLOS III

Case	Relevant Findings
Corfu Channel Case (United Kingdom v. Albania), 1949 ICJ Rep. 4 (9 April)	Straits used for international navigation
Anglo-Norwegian Fisheries Case, 1951, ICJ Rep. 116, 128-43 (18 December)	Articles 7(1), 7(3), 7(5) (straight baselines)
North Sea Continental Shelf Cases (Federated Republic of Germany v. Denmark; Federal Republic of Germany v. Netherlands), 1969 ICJ Rep. 3, 22, 25, 27, 29, 32-33, 38-40, 45 (20 February)	1958 Continental Shelf Convention Articles 1-5; 1958 High Seas Convention Preamble
Case Concerning Delimitation of the Maritime Boundary in the Gulf of Maine Area (Canada v. United States), 1984 ICJ Rep. 246, 294 (12 October)	Exclusive economic zone regime
Case Concerning the Continental Shelf (Libya v. Malta), 1985 ICJ Rep. 13, 33 (3 June)	Articles 57 breadth of the EEZ, 76(1) definition of the continental shelf, 83(1) delimitation
Case Concerning Military and Paramilitary Activities in and Against Nicaragua (Nicaragua v. United States), 1986 ICJ Rep. 14, 111-12 (27 June)	Articles 18 meaning of passage, and 58 rights and duties of other states in the EEZ
Case Concerning the Land, Island, and Maritime Frontier Dispute (El Salvador v. Honduras; Nicaragua intervening), 1992 ICJ Rep. 351, 588 (11 September)	Article 10 bays
Case Concerning Maritime Delimitation in the Area Between Greenland and Jan Mayen (Denmark v. Norway), 1993 ICJ Rep. 38, 58, 59, 62 (14 June)	1958 Continental Shelf Convention Article 6 on delimitation
Maritime Delimitation and Territorial Question Between Qatar and Bahrain (Qatar v. Bahrain), 2001 ICJ Rep. 40, 93, 94, 97, 101, 110, 111 (16 March)	Articles 2(1) legal status of territorial sea, 7(4) straight baselines, 13(1) low-tide elevations, 15 delimitation, 17 right of innocent passage, 74(1) and 83(1) delimitation, 12(2) islands; Articles 4(3), 11(1), 12(1), 14 of the 1958 Territorial Sea Convention
The Mox Plant Case (Ireland v. United Kingdom), Provisional Measures, ITLOS Order, para. 82 (December 3, 2001)	Duty to cooperate in Part XII
Case Concerning Land Reclamation by Singapore in and around the Straits of Johar (Malaysia v. Singapore), Provisional Measures, ITLOS Order, para. 92 (October 8, 2003)	Duty to cooperate Part XII
Territorial and Maritime Dispute (Nicaragua v. Colombia), 2012 ICJ Rep. 1, 43, 50, 51, 66, 111 (19 November)	Articles 2(1) legal status of territorial sea, 3 breadth of territorial sea, 5 normal baseline, 74(1) delimitation, 76(1) definition of continental shelf, 83(1) delimitation, 121 regime of islands; Articles 1(1) and 2 (sovereign over territorial sea) Territorial Sea Convention
Maritime Dispute (Peru v. Chile), 2014 ICJ Rep. para. 179 (27 January)	Articles 74(1) and 83(1) delimitation

Table VII.2: Cases Identifying Customary Norms Not in LOS Treaties

Case	**Relevant Findings**
Case Concerning Military and Paramilitary Activities in and Against Nicaragua (Nicaragua v. United States), 1986 ICJ Rep. 14, paras. 190-91 (27 June)	Use of force
The M/V "Saiga" (No. 2) Case (Saint Vincent and the Grenadines v. Guinea), ITLOS judgement, para. 155 (1 July 1999)	Use of force in maritime law enforcement
Southern Bluefin Tuna Cases (New Zealand v. Japan; Australia v. Japan), Provisional Measures, ITLOS, sep. op. Judge Laing, para, 16 and note 6 (August 27, 1999)	Precautionary principle not customary international law
Guyana v. Suriname, Decision of Annex VII Arbitral Panel, paras. 405-6, 445 (September 17, 2007)	Use of force
Pulp Mills on the River Uruguay (Argentina v. Uruguay), Judgement, 2010, ICJ Rep. 14, 83, para. 204 (20 April)	Environmental assessment required
The ARA Libertad Case (Argentina v. Ghana), ITLOS Order on request for provisional measures, para. 95 (Case No. 20, December 15, 2012)	Sovereign immunity of warships
The M/V "Virginia G" Case (Panama v. Guinea Bissau), ITLOS Judgement, 49, para. 153 (Case No. 19, April 14, 2014)	Exhaustion of local remedies as a prerequisite for diplomatic protect

Various commentators and legal experts as well as states have voiced their opinion on these questions. For instance, the United States addressed the first question by stating, "The Convention contains provisions with respect to traditional uses of the oceans [such as navigation and overflight] which generally confirm existing maritime law and practice."[15] In the late 1980s, the United States and the Soviet Union declared that the LOS Convention "with respect to the traditional uses of the oceans, generally constitutes international law and practice."[16] The International Law Association (ILA) and the International Law Commission (ILC) have examined various aspects of customary international law. In 2000, at its sixtieth Conference that took place in London, the ILA implemented a "Statement of Principles Applicable to the Formation of General Customary International Law."[17] The ILC analyzed the subject "Identification of Customary International Law" and its impact on states.[18]

The ICJ, recently, has had to confront the relationship between customary international law and the law of the sea because, in a number of highly publicized cases, some states had not consented to be bound by the relevant instrument. The Court was compelled to choose what provisions of the 1958 or 1982 Conventions were considered customary international law and therefore binding on states that could declare themselves persistent objectors.[19]

Regarding the persistent objection to the Convention, Turkey and Venezuela are notable examples. Each state regularly voted against the annual UN General Assembly resolution concerning oceans and the law of the sea. Turkey's explanation of its objection reads in part:

> In our opinion, the Convention does not provide sufficient safeguards for special geographical situations, and, as a consequence, does not take into consideration conflicting interesting and sensitivities arising from special circumstances. Furthermore, the Convention does not allow states to register reservations to its articles. Although we agree with the Convention in its general intent and with most of its provisions, we are unable to become a party to it owing to those prominent shortcomings. That being the case, we cannot support a resolution that calls on states to become parties to the United Nations Convention on the Law of the Sea and to harmonize their national legislation with its provisions.[20]

In *Qatar v. Bahrain*[21] and *Nicaragua v. Colombia*,[22] Qatar and Colombia were not party to UNCLOS III, whereas Bahrain and Nicaragua were. Neither Qatar nor Bahrain was party to the 1958 Conventions, whereas Nicaragua did not become a signatory to any of the 1958 Conventions, and Colombia only signed the Convention on the Continental Shelf.

It is noteworthy that, except for the North Sea Continental Shelf Cases,[23] 1969, the ICJ has not explained why certain specific provisions of UNCLOS III meet the standards for customary international law: "international custom, as evidenced by a practice generally accepted as law."[24] As will be seen below, the Court has acknowledged that only certain treaty provisions may be customary international law, or they may not be.

The Exclusive Economic Zone and Customary International Law

In the 1980s, a Chamber of the ICJ ruled that the EEZ concept was, indeed, customary international law.[1] Later, in the *Libya v. Malta Case*,[2] the full Court made a similar ruling. In the *Libya* case, the Court further held that Article 57 is also customary international law.[3] The ICJ, in the 1986 *Nicaragua v. United States* case, ruled that high seas navigational freedoms apply to the EEZ, as determined by Article 58.[4] In 2012, a decision by the ICJ held that the delimitation provisions of Article 74(1) represented customary international law.[5] The U.S. supports the notion that military survey activities in the EEZ are compatible with customary international law as a high seas freedom of navigation.[6]

James Crawford asserts that in 2012, "the EEZ forms part of customary law... The customary law version of the concept closely relates to the version that emerged in UNCLOS III. Under UNCLOS and customary law, the zone is optional and its existence depends on an actual claim."[7] Crawford observed that "many high seas freedoms are applicable in the EEZ (Articles 58, 86), and this is also the position in customary international law."[8]

Concerning the EEZ and as expressed in Part V of the LOS Convention, Churchill and Lowe observed that:

> What is part of customary international law are the broad rights of coastal and other states enumerated in articles 56 and 58 of the Convention. It is much more doubtful whether the detailed obligations in the articles relating to the exercise of coastal state jurisdiction over fisheries, pollution, and research have passed or are likely to quickly pass into customary international law, partly because of a lack of claims embodying the duties of the Convention, partly because there is some divergence between state practice and the Convention, and partly because some of the conventional rules would not seem to have the 'fundamentally norm-creating character' necessary for the creation of a rule of customary international law.[9]

When it comes to fisheries, the same authors note that:

> What is much less certain is whether the coastal state's fishery management duties set out in articles 61 and 62 have become part of customary law.[10]

Most of the twenty or so states that still claim or in the past have claimed a 200-mile exclusive fishing zone claim the jurisdiction to control fisheries research in the zone where it involves the taking of fish... It is likely that in general such claims now represent a rule of customary international law, first because there have been no protests to such claims (so far as we are aware), and secondly, because similar claims made in respect of twelve-mile exclusive fishing zones were... generally accepted.[11]

Crawford asserted that "the concept of preferential fishing rights seems to have survived in customary law" regardless of its absence from UNCLOS III.[12] The U.S. asserted that salmon fishing on the high seas, as expressed in Article 66(3), represents the core principles of customary international law.[13]

Concerning the rights of GDS and LLS to exploit the living resources of the EEZ, one commentator observed that "in light of the paucity of state practice on this subject, it remains uncertain whether and to what extent Articles 69–72 of LOSC have become customary international law."[14]

The High Seas

The ICJ has not examined the issue of the status of customary international law as it pertains to the provisions of Part VII, "The High Seas," of UNCLOS III. However, the Second Preambular paragraph of the 1958 High Seas Convention provides that its guidelines correlate with the "established principles of international law."[15] The Court has concluded that Article 2 regarding the freedoms of the seas represents customary international law.[16]

The guidelines of the High Seas Convention are reflected in Section 1 of Part VII, Articles 86–115, of the LOS Convention:

1. Article 87—freedom of the high seas (the High Seas Convention, Article 2);[17]
2. Article 89—invalidity of sovereignty claims over the high seas (Article 2, first sentence of the High Seas Convention);[18]
3. Article 90—right of navigation (Article 4 of the High Seas Convention);
4. Article 91—nationality of ships (Article 5 of the High Sea Convention);[19]
5. Article 92—status of ships (Article 6 of the High Seas Convention);[20]
6. Article 93—ships flying the UN flag (Article 7 of the High Seas Convention);
7. Article 94—duties of the flag state (Article 5(1) and 10 of the High Seas Convention);[21]
8. Article 95—immunity of warships on the high seas (Article 8 of the High Seas Convention);[22]
9. Article 96—immunity of ships used only on government noncommercial service (Article 9 of the High Seas Convention);
10. Article 97—penal jurisdiction in collisions (Article 11 of the High Seas Convention);
11. Article 98—duty to render assistance (Article 12 of High Seas Convention);
12. Article 99—prohibition of transport of slaves (Article 13 of the High Seas Convention);
13. Articles 100-107—piracy (Article 14-20 of the High Seas Convention);[23]
14. Article 110—right of visit (Article 22 of the High Seas Convention);[24]
15. Article 111—right of pursuit (Article 23 of the High Seas Convention);[25] and
16. Articles 112-15—submarine cables and pipelines (Articles 26-29 of the High Seas Convention).

The United States stated that Article 92 of the LOS Convention, along with Article 6 of the High Seas Conventions, codifies customary international law.[26] The United States noted that the semantics of Article 110 are customary international law.[27]

The ITLOS, in the M/V "Saiga" Case, provided that:

> Although the Convention does not contain express provisions on the use of force in the arrest of ships, international law, which is applicable by virtue of Article 293 of the Convention, requires that the use of force must be avoided as far as possible and, where force is unavoidable,

> it must not go beyond what is reasonable and necessary in the circumstances.[28]

One author noted that "insofar as jurisdiction is concerned, UNCLOS Part VII generally reflects customary international law," commenting specifically on Articles 88–90, 92(1), and 94.[29] This same author observed that "custom has come to reflect" piracy as defined by Article 101,[30] and that the right of approach, although not mentioned in UNCLOS Part VII, is considered customary international law.[31]

Other commenters support the notion that the right of "ships to enter the territorial sea on a temporary basis to provide assistance to vessels in distress or persons in jeopardy at sea" exists under customary international law, in Articles 18(2) and 98 of the LOS Convention and the Safety of Life at Sea Convention.[32] Crawford provides that the "freedom of fishing on the high seas was well established in customary international law," but is qualified by the conditions put forth in the LOS Convention Part VII, Section 2.[33]

Submarine Cables

The ICJ declared, in the *North Sea Continental Shelf Cases*, that Article 4 of the 1958 Continental Shelf Convention was customary international law.[34] The Court also ruled that the Preamble to the High Seas Convention is compatible with the standards of international law.[35] The issue of submarine cables is addressed in Articles 26-29 of the High Seas Convention. The provisions of the LOS Convention that pertain to submarine cables, Articles 21(1)(c), 51(2), 58(1), 79, 87(1)(c), 112-15, and 297(1)(a), have not been examined by the international courts to determine if they correlate to customary norms. In the book *Submarine Cables: the Handbook of Law and Policy*, the authors asserted that "most of the provisions of UNCLOS (including the provisions on submarine cables) can be said to bind non-parties as they are best evidence of customary law."[36]

The Regime of Islands

In the *Nicaragua v. Colombia* Case, the ICJ reasoned that the three paragraphs of Article 121 pertaining to the regime of the islands are customary norms.[37]

Landlocked and Geographically Disadvantaged States

The customary international status of various provisions relating to LLS and GDS contained in the LOS Convention has not been analyzed by the courts and tribunals. One author noted that navigational freedom relating to the navigational rights of LLS "can reasonably be considered as part of customary international law."[38]

Marine Pollution

The ICJ has noted that the "general obligation of states to ensure that activities under their jurisdiction and control respect the environment or other states or of areas beyond national control is now a part of the corpus of international law relating to the environment."[39] The rule mirrors Article 194(2) of the LOS Convention, which is considered customary international law.[40]

ITLOS has stated that "the duty to cooperate is a fundamental principle in the prevention of pollution of the marine environment under Part XII of the Convention and general international law and that rights arise therefrom which the Tribunal may consider appropriate to preserve under 290 of the Convention."[41]

The ICJ has ruled that "it may now be considered a requirement under general international law to undertake an environmental assessment where there is a risk that the proposed industrial activity may have a significantly adverse impact in a transboundary context, in particular, on a shared resource."[42] This obligation is reflected in Article 206, Assessment of potential effects of activities of the LOS Convention. Judges Laing and Wolfrum believe that the precautionary principle is not representative of customary international law.[43]

Churchill and Lowe note that the following provisions in Part XII of the LOS Convention reflect customary international law:

1. Article 210(5)—dumping within the territorial sea, EEZ, and onto the shelf;[44]
2. Article 221—intervention beyond the territorial sea;[45] and
3. Article 236—sovereign immunity.[46]

These two authors further observed, "In light of this limited and somewhat divergent practice, it must be doubtful whether those provisions of the Law of the Sea Convention relating to coastal and port state jurisdiction in respect of ships which go beyond the traditional law have become part of customary international law."[47]

Tanaka studied the relationship between customary international law and marine environmental protection prior to 1982[48] and under the LOS Convention.[49] Concerning the LOS Convention, Tanaka said, "there maybe room for the view that obligations for the protection of the marine environment embodied in the LOSC have become part of customary law."[50] He further asserted that the duty to notify that is a part of Article 198 may already fit the requirements of customary international law.[51] The final report of the ILA's Committee on Coastal State Jurisdiction Relating to Marine Pollution states that the terms "generally accepted international rules and standards [located within Articles

21(4), 211(2), 211(5), 211(6)(c), and 226(1)(a)] cannot be equated with customary international law."[52]

Marine Scientific Research

Although the various international courts and tribunals have not addressed the customary international law status of the provisions on MSR contained in Part XIII of the LOS Convention, the U.S. supports the notion that the right to regulate MSR in the territorial sea contained in Article 21(1)(g) of the LOS Convention is customary international law.[53]

Churchill and Lowe commented upon this issue by observing:

> The principle of coastal state consent for research in the EEZ and on the continental shelf is now part of customary international law. However, many of the details of the Convention regime, such as the period of notice and implied consent, are not now, and are probably incapable of becoming part of customary international law because of the paucity of state practice and because they do not seem to have the fundamentally norm-creating character necessary an emergent rule of customary law.[54]

Table of Cases

Case Title	Citation
Anglo-Norwegian Fisheries Case (United Kingdom v. Norway)	ICJ Rep. 116 (1951)
Asylum Case (Colombia v. Peru)	ICJ Rep. 266 (1950)
Barcelona Traction, Light and Power Company Ltd Case	ICJ Rep. (1970)
Case Concerning Delimitation of the Maritime Boundary in the Gulf of Maine Area (Canada v. United States)	ICJ Rep. 246, 294 (1984)
Case Concerning Land Reclamation by Singapore (Malaysia v. Singapore)	ITLOS Order, para. 92 (2003)
Case Concerning Military and Paramilitary Activities in and Against Nicaragua (Nicaragua v. United States)	ICJ Rep. 14 (1986)
Case Concerning the Continental Shelf (Libya v. Malta)	ICJ Rep. 13 (1985)
Case Concerning the Land, Island and Maritime Frontier Dispute (El Salvador v. Honduras; Nicaragua intervening)	ICJ Rep. 351 (1992)
Case Concerning Maritime Delimitation in the Area Between Greenland and Jan Mayen (Denmark v. Norway)	ICJ Rep. 38 (1993)
Corfu Channel Case (United Kingdom v. Albania)	ICJ Rep. 4 (1949)
The Gulf of Maine Case (Canada v. United States)	ICJ Rep. 246 (1984)
Guyana v. Suriname	Arbitral Panel Decision (2007)
Island of Palmas Case (United States v. Netherlands)	PCA Award (1928), II RIAA 829
Maritime Delimitation and Territorial Question Between Qatar and Bahrain (Qatar v. Bahrain)	ICJ Rep. 40 (2001)
Maritime Dispute (Peru v. Chile)	ICJ Rep. (2014)
The Minquiers and Ecrehos Case	ICJ Rep. (1953)
The Mox Plant Case (Ireland v. United Kingdom)	ITLOS Order, para. 82 (2001)
The M/V "Saiga" (No. 2) Case (Saint Vincent and the Grenadines v. Guinea)	ITLOS Judgement, para. 155 (1999)
The M/V "Virginia G" Case (Panama v. Guinea Bissau)	ITLOS Judgement, para. 153 (2014)
The North Sea Continental Shelf Cases	ICJ Rep. (1969)

Nottebohm Case	ICJ Rep. (1955)
Nuclear Tests Case	ICJ Rep. (1974)
Pulp Mills on the River Uruguay (Argentina v. Uruguay)	ICJ Rep. 14 (2010)
Right of Passage Over Indian Territory Case (Portugal v. India)	ICJ Rep. (1960)
Southern Bluefin Tuna Cases (New Zealand v. Japan; Australia v. Japan)	ITLOS, Provisional Measures (1999)
SS Lotus Case (France v. Turkey)	PCIJ, Series A, No. 10 (1927)
Temple of Preah Vihear Case (Cambodia v. Thailand)	ICJ Rep. 6 (1962)
Territorial and Maritime Dispute (Nicaragua v. Colombia)	ICJ Rep. 1 (2012)
The ARA Libertad Case (Argentina v. Ghana)	ITLOS Order, para. 95 (2012)
US Nationals in Morocco Case (United States v. France)	ICJ Rep. (1952)
US Diplomatic and Consular Staff in Tehran Case	ICJ Rep. (1980)

Endnotes by Chapter

Introduction

1. N.C.H., "The Myth of Customary International Law," Australian Yearbook of International Law 1 (1983); Patrick Kelly, "The Twilight of Customary International Law," Virginia Journal of International Law 40 (2000): 449.

Chapter I: The International and Geo-Political Systems

1. A. Kiss and D. Shelton, "Systems Analysis of International Law: A Methodological Inquiry," Netherlands Yearbook of International Law (1986): 45-50.
2. R. Coate et al., "Interdependence in International Organization and Global Governance."
3. Ibid.
4. H. Milner, "The Assumption of Anarchy in International Relations Theory: A Critique," in International Organization and Global Governance: A Reader, ed. F. Kratochwil and E. D. Mansfield (2006): 4-19.
5. Ibid., 15.
6. Ibid.
7. R. Axelrod and R. O. Keohane, "Achieving Cooperation under Anarchy: Strategies and Institutions," World Politics 38, no. 1 (1985): 226-254.
8. K. Waltz, Theory of International Politics (Reading, MA: Addison-Wesley, 1979), 80-101.
9. R. Axelrod and R. Keohane, "Achieving Cooperation under Anarchy: Strategies and Institutions," World Politics 38, no. 1 (1985): 226.
10. H. Bull, The Anarchical Society (London: Macmillan, 1977), 16-19.
11. "International politics is a struggle for power. Power is the immediate aim." H. Morgenthau, Politics among Nations (New York: Knopf, 1948), 13-14.
12. David Hume suggests that men could submit themselves to behavioral limits when it is common to sustain their interests: "It is only a general sense of common interest... which induces them to regulate their conduct by certain rules..." D. Hume, A Treatise of Human Nature (Oxford: Clarendon Press, 1960), 490.
13. Waltz, Theory of International Politics, 107.
14. In essence, the existence of international institutions reflects the overall participation of States within the international system.

15. Waltz gives a great example of this when he stated: "If one expects others to make a run on a bank, one's own prudent course is to run faster than they do even while knowing that if few others run, the bank will remain solvent, and if many run, it will fail. In such cases, pursuit of individual interest produces collective results that nobody wants, yet individuals by behaving differently will hurt themselves without altering outcomes." Waltz, Theory of International Politics, 107-108.
16. R. Aron, Paix et guerre entre les Nations (Paris: Calmann-Lévy, 1962), 108.
17. Sovereign equality is enshrined in the UN Charter, and reaffirmed in the 1970 Declaration on Principles of International Law concerning Friendly Relations and Co-operation among States in accordance with the Charter of the United Nations (UN General Assembly Resolution 2625).
18. In essence, the international ordering system still has a long way to go in order to replicate the authority mechanism seen in domestic systems. B. Cheng, "Introduction to Subjects of International Law," in International Law: Achievement and Prospects, ed. M. Bedjaoui (Dordrecht: Martinus Nijhoff, 1991), 33-34.
19. It is not suggested that these characteristics make the international system ineffective in its objectives. Despite the inherent weaknesses of the international system, it is still unique when it comes to facilitating the inter-relationship between states.
20. I. Kant, Eternal Peace, trans. W. Hastie (Boston: American Peace Society, 1914), 30, 37.
21. The concept 'international community of States' is meant to include both co-operative efforts and conflict that arise between States.
22. See also the use of this expression by Denmark in I.C.J. Pleadings, North Sea Continental Shelf cases, Vol. I (The Hague: ICJ, 1968), 190.
23. H. Mosler, The International Society as a Legal Community (Dordrecht: Sijthoff & Noordhoff, 1980), 17-20.
24. K. Abbott, "Prospects for International Lawyers," Yale Journal of International Law 14 (1989): 344-246.
25. L. Henkin, How Nations Behave, 2nd ed. (New York: Columbia University Press, 1979), 15.
26. A. D'Amato, "Is International Law Really Law?" in International Law, ed. M. Koskenniemi (Aldershot: Dartmouth, 1992), 39-41.
27. The conflict between a State's objectives and its needs and the requirements of the international system is important.
28. The common heritage of mankind principle is a prime representative of this. It is not intended here to classify these two groups of rules according

to their normative value (for instance, whether one set of rules represents jus cogens or not) or examine their hierarchy.

29. M. Mendelson, "Fragmentation of the Law of the Sea," Marine Policy 12 (1988): 192-200.

Chapter II: Article 38 of the Statute of the Permanent Court of International Justice

Historical Background

1. This Committee was composed of Mr. Adatci (Japan), Mr. Altamira (Spain), Mr. Bevilacqua (Brazil, who was later replaced by Mr. Fernandes), Baron Descamps (Belgium), Mr. Hagerup (Norway), Mr. de Lapradelle (France), Mr. Loder (Netherlands), Lord Phillimore (United Kingdom), Mr. Rucci-Busatti (Italy), and Mr. Root (United States).
2. Permanent Court of International Justice, Advisory Committee of Jurists, Documents Presented to the Committee Relating to Existing Plans for the Establishment of a Permanent Court of International Justice (The Hague: PCIJ, 1920), 179.
3. Process-Verbaux of the Proceedings of the Advisory Committee of Jurists, July 16th- July 24th, with annexes (The Hague: PCIJ, 1920), 89.
4. Permanent Court of International Justice, Documents Presented to the Committee, 267.
5. Ibid., 97.
6. Ibid., 146-147.
7. Process-Verbaux of the Proceedings, 295.
8. Ibid., 306.
9. Ibid., 344.
10. Ibid., 351.
11. Ibid., 548.
12. Ibid., 636, 680.
13. The League of Nations, Permanent Court of International Justice, Documents Concerning the Action Taken by the Council of the League of Nations under Article 14 of the Covenant (Geneva: League of Nations, 1921), 68.
14. There is no comment regarding the Sub-Committee's rejection of Argentina's proposal. Ibid., 145.
15. Ibid., 219.
16. Ibid., 257.

17. League of Nations, Committee of Jurists on the Statute of the Permanent Court of International Justice, Minutes of the Session held at Geneva (Final Report) (Geneva: League of Nations, 1929), 124.
18. Ibid., 219.
19. Process-Verbaux of the Proceedings, 322.
20. J. Brown Scott, ed., Selection from Three Works of Francisco Suarez, in The Classics of International Law (Oxford: Clarendon Press, 1944), 441-442.
21. Ibid., 445-448.
22. Process-Verbaux of the Proceedings, 293-295, 584.
23. Ibid., 729.
24. Ibid.
25. H. Bonfils, Manuel de Droit International Public, 8th ed. (Paris: Arthur Rousseau, 1914), 24-25; P. Fauchille, Traité de Droit International Public (Paris: Arthur Rousseau, 1922), 42-43.
26. Process-Verbaux of the Proceedings, 294-295.

Doctrinal Interpretations

1. Karol Wolfke, Custom in Present International Law (Dordrecht: Martinus Nijhoff, 1964), 18.
2. Hans Kelsen, The Law of the United Nations (London: Stevens & Sons, 1951), 533.
3. Documents of the United Nations Conference on International Organizations, United Nations Committee of Jurists, UN Information Organizations, vol. XIV (San Francisco: United Nations, 1945), 435-436.
4. See, for instance, Permanent Court of International Justice, Series D. n.6, Collection of Texts Governing the Jurisdiction of the Court (Leiden: A.W. Sijthoff, 1932), 75, 160, 183, 187, and 289.

Chapter III: State Consent and International Customary Law

Value-oriented Customary International Law

1. J. Tasioulas, "Opinio Juris and the Genesis of Custom: A Solution to the Paradox," Australian Yearbook of International Law 26 (2007): 199-205.

The Need for State Consent

1. G. Palmer, "New Ways to Make Environmental Law," American Journal of International Law 86 (1992): 259.
2. A. Guzman, How International Law Works: A Rational Choice Theory (Oxford: Oxford University Press, 2008), 172-73.

3. E. Rosand, "The Security Council as Global Legislator: Ultra Vires or Ultra Innovative?" Fordham International Law Journal 28 (2005): 542, 575-76.
4. United Nations Charter, art. 42.
5. Rome Statute, International Criminal Court (2023).
6. E. S. Edelman et al., "The Dangers of NATO a Nuclear Iran," Foreign Affairs 90, no. 1 (2011): 66-81.
7. Guzman, How International Law Works, 42-45.
8. T. Franck, Fairness in International Law and Institutions (Oxford: Oxford University Press, 1995).
9. J. Brunnée and S. Toope, Legitimacy and Legality in International Law: An Interactional Account (Cambridge: Cambridge University Press, 2010).
10. Franck, Fairness in International Law and Institutions.
11. Ibid., 30-45.
12. Ibid., 25-46.
13. K. Alter, "Delegation to International Courts: Self-Binding vs. Other-Binding Delegation," Law and Contemporary Problems 71 (2008): 37; Eric Posner and John C. Yoo, "Judicial Independence in International Tribunals," California Law Review 93 (2005): 1; Laurence R. Helfer and Anne-Marie Slaughter, "Toward a Theory of Effective Supranational Adjudication," Yale Law Journal 107 (1997): 273.
14. Ibid.
15. J. Jackson, "International Law Status of WTO Dispute Settlement Reports: Obligations to Comply or Option to 'Buy Out'?" American Journal of International Law 98 (2004): 109.
16. Michael Nicholson, Rationality and the Analysis of International Conflict (Cambridge: Cambridge University Press, 1992), 56.
17. Emmerich De Vattel, The Law of Nations (Philadelphia: T. & J.W. Johnson, 1982), ixvi; Christian Wolff, Methodo Scientifica Petratatum, ed. James Brown Scott, The Classics of International Law, Vol. II (Oxford: Clarendon Press, 1934), 6, 11, 12, 17.

The Autolimitation Theory

1. H.L.A. Hart, The Concept of Law, 2nd ed. (Oxford: Oxford University Press, 1991), 219.
2. H. Lauterpacht, Private Law Sources and Analogies of International Law (London: Longmans, Green and Co., 1927), 56.
3. John Rawls, A Theory of Justice (Cambridge, MA: Harvard University Press, 1991), 244-245.

4. Richard Tuck, ed., Thomas Hobbes, Leviathan (Cambridge: Cambridge University Press, 1991), 91.
5. Ibid.
6. Ibid., 91-92.
7. Ibid.
8. G. Fitzmaurice, "The Law and Procedure of the International Court of Justice, 1951-54: General Principles and Sources of Law," British Yearbook of International Law 30 (1953): 9-12.
9. Julius Stone, Of Law and Nations (Buffalo, NY: William S. Hein, 1974), 71-118.
10. J.L. Brierly, The Basis of Obligation in International Law (Oxford: Clarendon Press, 1958), 6-9.
11. J. Raz, The Concept of a Legal System (Oxford: Clarendon Press, 1970), 31.
12. H.L.A. Hart, The Concept of Law, 2nd ed. (Oxford: Oxford University Press, 1991), 218.

The Theory of Collective Will

1. Jean-Jacques Rousseau, "Perpetual Peace," in Collected Writings of Rousseau, ed. Roger D. Masters and Christopher Kelly (Hanover, NH: University Press of New England, 2005), 42.
2. Jean-Jacques Rousseau, On the Social Contract, trans. D. Cress (Indianapolis: Hackett Publishing, 1987), 7, 20, 24.
3. Ibid., 26.
4. ILC, Draft Conclusions on the Identification of Customary International Law, UN Doc A/73/10, YBILC 11, General Commentary 3 (2018).
5. Some jus cogens norms may instead be 'general principles of law'; Draft Articles on Responsibility of States for Internationally Wrongful Acts with Commentaries, UN Doc A/56/10, YBILC 31 (2001).
6. A.T. Guzman and J. Hsiang, "Reinvigorating Customary International Law," in Custom's Future: International Law in a Changing World, ed. C.A. Bradley (Cambridge: Cambridge University Press, 2016); L. Helfer and I. Wuerth, "Customary International Law: An Instrumental Choice Perspective," Michigan Journal of International Law 37, no. 4 (2016): 563.
7. J. Trachtman, "The Growing Obsolescence of Customary International Law," in Custom's Future: International Law in a Changing World, ed. C.A. Bradley (Cambridge: Cambridge University Press, 2016).
8. H.L.A. Hart, Punishment and Responsibility: Essays in Philosophy of Law (Oxford: Oxford University Press, 1968), 28; T.M. Scanlon, "The Significance of Choice," The Tanner Lectures on Human Values 7 (1986): 149, 211.

9. N. Krisch, "The Decay of Consent: International Law in the Age of Global Public Goods," American Journal of International Law 108, no. 1 (2014): 1.
10. Y. Shany, "Assessing the Effectiveness of International Courts: A Goal-Based Approach," American Journal of International Law 106, no. 2 (2012): 225, 241.
11. T. Christiano, "Climate Change and State Consent," in Climate Change and Justice, ed. J. Moss (Oxford: Oxford University Press, 2015), 22.
12. M. Byers, Custom, Power and the Power of Rules: International Relations and Customary International Law, ch. 9 (Cambridge: Cambridge University Press, 1999).
13. A. Pellet, "The Normative Dilemma: Will and Consent in International Law-Making," Australian Yearbook of International Law 12 (1989): 22; E. Posner, "Do States Have a Moral Obligation to Obey International Law?" Stanford Law Review 55, no. 5 (2003): 1901, 1910-11.
14. K. Wolfke, Custom in Present International Law (Dordrecht: Martinus Nijhoff, 1993).
15. J. Locke, Two Treatises of Government, 2nd treatise, ch. 8, 119 (London: Awnsham Churchill, 1690).
16. Wolfke, Custom in Present International Law, 97.
17. International Law Commission, Draft Conclusions on the Identification of Customary International Law, UN Doc A/73/10 (2018).
18. T. Bodansky, "The Legitimacy of International Governance: A Coming Challenge for International Environmental Law?" American Journal of International Law 93, no. 3 (1999): 596; M. Zürn, "Global Governance and Legitimacy Problems," Government and Opposition 39, no. 2 (2004): 260; A. Buchanan and R.O. Keohane, "The Legitimacy of Global Governance Institutions," Ethics and International Affairs 20, no. 4 (2006): 405, 412-14.
19. N. Roughan, "Sources and the Normativity of International Law: From Validity to Justification," in The Oxford Handbook on the Sources of International Law, ed. S. Besson and J. d'Aspremont (Oxford: Oxford University Press, 2017), 680; O. Suttle, "Rules and Values in International Adjudication: The Case of the WTO Appellate Body," International and Comparative Law Quarterly 68, no. 2 (2019): 399.

Complications of State Consent

1. Vienna Convention on the Law of Treaties, art. 52 (1969).
2. Ibid., art. 75.
3. Ibid., art. 53; ILC, CIL Conclusions 8.

4. A. Peters, "Global Constitutionalism Revisited," International Legal Theory 11 (2005): 39, 51; M. Fitzmaurice, "Third Parties and the Law of the Treaties," Max Planck Yearbook of United Nations Law 6, no. 1 (2002): 37; J. Alvarez, International Organizations as Law-Makers (Oxford: Oxford University Press, 2006); I. Venzke, How Interpretation Makes International Law: On Semantic Change and Normative Twists (Oxford: Oxford University Press, 2012); E. Fahey, The Actors of Postnational Rule-Making: Contemporary Challenges of European and International Law (London: Routledge, 2017); ILA Committee on Formation of Customary (General) International Law, Final Report of the Committee: Statement of Principles Applicable to the Formation of General Customary International Law Principle 10 and its accompanying commentary (2000); C. Tomuschat, "Obligations Arising for States Without or Against Their Will," Collected Courses of the Hague Academy of International Law 241 (1993): 262-64.
5. ILC, Fourth Report on the Law of Treaties by Gerald Fitzmaurice, Special Rapporteur, UN Doc A/CN.4/120 (1959).
6. VCLT, arts 53 & 64.
7. Ibid.
8. S. Ratner, The Thin Justice of International Law: Moral Reckoning of the Law of Nations (Oxford: Oxford University Press, 2015), 4; T. Christiano, "Is Democratic Legitimacy Possible for International Institutions?" in Global Democracy: Normative and Empirical Perspectives, ed. D. Archibugi et al. (Cambridge: Cambridge University Press, 2011), 69.
9. A. Guzman, "Against Consent," Virginia Journal of International Law 52, no. 4 (2012): 747.
10. For further discussion on these questions see A. Buchanan, Justice, Legitimacy, and Self-Determination: Moral Foundations for International Law (Oxford: Oxford University Press, 2003), 301; T. Christiano, "Ronald Dworkin, State Consent, and Progressive Cosmopolitanism," in The Legacy of Ronald Dworkin, ed. W. Waluchow and S. Sciaraffa (Oxford: Oxford University Press, 2016), 49.
11. H.L.A. Hart, Punishment and Responsibility: Essays in the Philosophy of Law (Oxford: Oxford University Press, 1968), 44-45; Christiano, "Is Democratic Legitimacy Possible"; R. Dworkin, "A New Philosophy for International Law," Philosophy & Public Affairs 41, no. 1 (2013): 2, 10.
12. S. Besson, The Morality of Conflict: Reasonable Disagreement and the Law (Oxford: Hart Publishing, 2005), 459.
13. Charter of the United Nations, 1 UNTS XVI, 4, art. 2(1) (1945).
14. L. Oppenheim, International Law -- Vol 1: Peace, 8th ed. (London: Longmans, 1955), 263. (emphasis added).

15. S. Besson, "State Consent and Disagreement in International Law-Making," Leiden Journal of International Law 29, no. 2 (2016): 289, 292.
16. A. Buchanan, "Institutional Legitimacy," in Oxford Studies in Political Philosophy, vol. 4, ed. D. Sobel et al. (Oxford: Oxford University Press, 2018), 57.
17. N. Krisch, "The Decay of Consent: International Law in an Age of Global Public Goods," American Journal of International Law 108, no. 1 (2014): 1.

Chapter IV: State Practice

An Overview of National Digests and the Concept of State Practice

1. In the descriptions of the contents of the digests, uniform and general terms have been used as much as possible. For instance, the words 'Government' or 'Governmental' cover all organs of the Executive, not only the Foreign Office or Ministry of Foreign Affairs. Likewise, diplomatic notes or diplomatic correspondence consist not only of correspondence between a given Foreign Office and its diplomatic corps, but also correspondence of Heads of State.
2. Council of Europe, Publication of Digests of State Practice in the Field of Public International Law (Strasbourg: Council of Europe, 1970), 9-13.
3. Directory of French practice in matters of public international law. Translation by author.
4. A. Kiss, Repertoire de la pratique française en matière de droit international public (Paris: Centre National de la Recherche Scientifique, 1962), xiv.
5. A.A. Cançado Trindale, Repertório Brasileiro da Prática do Direito Internacional Público (Brasília: Fundação Alexandre de Gusmão, 1984).
6. Ibid.
7. P. Guggenheim, Repertoire Suisse de droit International Public, 1914-1939, ed. A. Bale (Geneva: Imprimerie du Journal de Genève, 1975), vol I, vii, ix.
8. Ibid.
9. N. Giuseppe, ed., The Italian Yearbook of International Law (Leiden: Brill Nijhoff, 2022).
10. Ibid.
11. Digest of United States Practice in International Law, 1989-2012 (Washington, DC: U.S. Department of State, 2021).
12. Ibid.
13. S. Swan, Australian Practice in International Law (Canberra: Australian National University Press, 2021).
14. Ibid.

15. The Japanese Annual of International Law (Tokyo: Japan Society of International Law, 2002).
16. Ibid.
17. J. H. Currie, "The Canadian Yearbook of International Law/Annuaire canadien de droit international: Founding, Function, Future," in Netherlands Yearbook of International Law, ed. O. Spijkers et al. (The Hague: T.M.C. Asser Press, 2021).
18. Ibid.
19. Ministry for Foreign Affairs, Government of Sweden (Stockholm: Ministry for Foreign Affairs, 2023).
20. Ibid.
21. The South Africa Yearbook of International Law (Pretoria: University of South Africa Press, 2023).
22. Ibid.
23. C. Parry, ed., A British Digest of International Law (London: Stevens & Sons, 1967).
24. Ibid.

An Examination of Case Law

1. Of all the cases presented, the Nuclear Tests case was the only one in which the Court did not proceed to examine the evidence produced because the case did not reach the merits.
2. The Asylum Case (Colombia v. Peru), ICJ Rep. 266 (1950).
3. The Right of Passage Case (Portugal v India), ICJ Rep. 6 (1960).
4. Case Concerning Rights of Nationals of the United States of America in Morocco (France v. United States), ICJ Rep. (1952).
5. Ibid.
6. North Sea Continental Shelf (Denmark/Federal Republic of Germany/ Netherlands), ICJ Rep. 1 (1969).
7. Ibid.
8. Ibid.
9. Nuclear Tests Case (Australia/New Zealand v. France), ICJ Rep. 253, 457 (1974).
10. Ibid.
11. Article 5 of the International Law Commission's Draft on State Responsibility and comments in Yearbook of the International Law Commission, vol. II, Part One (New York: United Nations, 1971), 233-238; H. Kelsen, Principles of International Law (New York: Rinehart, 1952), 117-118.

12. This belief is based upon the concept that custom is a form of tacit consent or implicit agreement.
13. Enumeration of such entities is contained in Art. 7(2) of the 1969 Vienna Convention on the Law of Treaties.
14. Even Tunkin, who holds a consensualist view in his coordination of wills' theory, highlights the difference between the customary and treaty process. G. Tunkin, "International Law in the International System," Recueil des Cours de l'Académie de Droit International 147 (1975): 128-129. On the tacit pact theory as it pertains to custom, see Chapter III, 39-46.
15. H. Lauterpacht, International Law, vol. I (Cambridge: Cambridge University Press, 1970), 67; C. Parry, "The Practice of States," The Grotius Society 44 (1959): 170; P. Guggenheim, Traité de droit International Public (Geneva: Georg, 1953), 50-52.
16. Ways and Means of Making the Evidence of Customary International Law More Readily Available, Memorandum submitted by the Secretary-General, United Nations, Doc A/CN.4/6 (1949).
17. Ibid.
18. There are different opinions concerning this requirement. For instance, Judge Nyholm, in the SS Lotus case, asserted that the acts of States must have been accomplished within the domain of international relations. The SS Lotus Case, PCIJ, Judgement (1927).
19. Ibid.
20. The Namibia Case, "Separate Opinion of Vice-President Ammoun" (1971).
21. Ibid.
22. For instance, when the State ratifies or authorizes the acts of private individuals. See Fisheries Case (United Kingdom v Norway), ICJ Rep. 3 (Diss. Opinion of Sir Arnold MacNair and Sep. Opinion of Judge Hsu Mo) (1951).
23. Article 5 of the International Law Commission's Draft on State Responsibility and comments in Yearbook of the International Law Commission (1971).
24. Ibid. According to the Report of the International Law Commission, in such exceptional cases as the individual acting as 'de facto official', he is performing a function "which should normally be performed by an organ of the State administration or of one of the other public institutions or entities, or is called upon to provide a service or perform a specific task on behalf of the State."
25. Yearbook of the International Law Commission, vol II (New York: United Nations, 1976), 75-79.

26. Concerning the treaty process, the organs or entities of the State which have the power to formally express the State's consent are those that are defined in Art. 7 of the Vienna Convention on the Law of Treaties.

The Scope of International Practice and Types of Custom

1. UN Doc.A/CN.4/16, Yearbook of the International Law Commission, Vol. II (New York: United Nations, 1950), 26.
2. Yearbook of the International Law Commission, Vol. I (New York: United Nations, 1950), 5.
3. Case Concerning Right of Passage Over Indian Territory, ICJ Rep. 39 (1960).
4. Colombian-Peruvian Asylum Case, Judgement ICJ Rep. (1950). (Judges Alvarez, Read, Azevedo, and Castilla acknowledged this sectional/regional custom).
5. Case Concerning Rights of Nationals of the United States of America in Morocco, ICJ Rep. 199-200 (1952).
6. Nottebohm Case, Judgement ICJ Rep. (1955).
7. Colombian-Peruvian Asylum Case, Judgement ICJ Rep. (1950).
8. Ibid.
9. Case Concerning Rights of Nationals of the United States of America in Morocco, Judgement ICJ Rep. (1952).
10. Case Concerning Right of Passage Over Indian Territory, Judgement ICJ Rep. (1960).
11. North Sea Continental Shelf Cases, ICJ Pleadings (1969).
12. Ibid.
13. H. Thierry, et al., Droit international Public (Paris: Montchrestien, 1984), 119-120; M. Akehurst, "Custom as a Source of International Law," British Yearbook of International Law 47 (1975).
14. In the Fisheries case, the Court pointed out that, for the purpose of measuring the breadth of the territorial sea, "it is the low-water mark... which has generally been adopted in the practice of States"; In the Corfu Channel case, a general custom on innocent passage through the straits had been recognized by the Court. The Corfu Channel Case, Judgement ICJ Rep. (1949).
15. The SS Wimbledon Case, PCIJ (1923).
16. North Sea Continental Shelf Cases, ICJ Reports (1969).
17. Ibid. (Dissenting Opinion of Judge Sorensen).
18. Ibid.

19. Yearbook of the International Law Commission, Vol. II (New York: United Nations, 1966), 248.

Lex Specialis Derogat Legi Generali

1. M. Koskenniemi, Study on the Function and Scope of the Lex Specialis Rule and the Question of "Self-Contained Regimes", UN Doc. ILC(LVI)/SG/FIL/CRD.1/Add.1 (2004).
2. Statute of the International Court of Justice, Article 38(1) (1945).
3. Statute of the Permanent Court of International Justice, Treaty Series 6 (1920), 390.
4. R. Wolfrum, "Sources of International Law," in Max Planck Encyclopedia of Public International Law (Oxford: Oxford University Press, 2011).
5. South West Africa (Ethiopia v. South Africa; Liberia v. South Africa), ICJ Rep. 6, at 47 (para. 88) (1966).
6. A. Pellet, "Article 38," in The Statute of the International Court of Justice, ed. A. Zimmerman et al. (Oxford: Oxford University Press, 2012), 731-870.
7. Ibid.
8. The principle lex specialis generalisbus derogat was one of the examples used during the drafting provision which became Article 38(1)(c) of the PCIJ. B. Cheng, General Principles of Law as Applied by International Courts and Tribunals (London: Stevens & Sons, 1954), 26.
9. Vienna Convention on the Law of Treaties, Articles 26 and 34 (1969).
10. This is in consideration that there is a possibility that some customary rules may be regarded as having the character of jus cogens.
11. Case Concerning United States Diplomatic and Consular Staff in Tehran, Judgement ICJ Rep. (1980); Reservations to the Genocide Convention, Advisory Opinion (1951).
12. A. Verdross, "Jus Dispositivum and Jus Cogens in International Law," American Journal of International Law 60 (1966): 55.
13. North Sea Continental Shelf Case, Judgment ICJ (1969).
14. P. Weil, "Towards Relative Normativity in International Law," American Journal of International Law 77 (1983): 413.
15. The customary rules pertaining to the non-use of force and non-intervention are, for example, universally established and are recognized as rules of jus cogens.

Customary International Law: Formation and Objection

1. North Sea Continental Shelf Cases, ICJ Rep. (1969); The Fisheries Jurisdiction Case (United Kingdom v. Iceland), Judgement ICJ Rep. (1974).

2. Ibid. (Separate Opinion of Judge Padilla Nervo).
3. Fisheries Case, Judgement ICJ Rep. (1951).
4. Military and Paramilitary Activities in and against Nicaragua Case, Judgement ICJ Rep. (1986).
5. Fisheries Case, Pleadings ICJ Rep. (1951).
6. This is according to the statement: "It does not at all follow that, in the absence of rules having the technically precise character alleged by the United Kingdom Government, the delimitation undertaken by the Norwegian Government in 1935 is not subject to certain principles which make it possible to judge as to its validity under international law." Ibid.
7. Nicaragua Case, Judgement ICJ Rep. (1986).
8. Ibid.
9. The Gulf of Maine Case, Judgement ICJ Rep. (1984).
10. Colombian-Peruvian Asylum Case, Judgement ICJ Rep. (1950).
11. Fisheries Case, Judgement ICJ Rep. (1951).
12. Ibid.
13. H. Grotius, De Juri Belli Ac Pacts Libri Tres, in The Classics of International Law, ed. J. Brown Scott (Oxford: Clarendon Press, 1925), 17, 44.
14. See the Asylum Case, Judgement ICJ Rep. (1950) (Dissenting Opinion of Judge Read and Dissenting Opinion of Judge Castilla); US Nationals in Morocco Case, Judgement ICJ Rep. (1952).
15. UN Doc, A/CN.4/16, Yearbook of the International Law Commission, vol. II (New York: United Nations, 1950), 26.
16. North Sea Continental Shelf Cases, Judgement ICJ rep. (Dissenting Opinion Judge Tanaka) (1969).
17. Case Concerning Right of Passage Over Indian Territory, Judgement ICJ Rep. (Judge Armand-Ugon) (1960).
18. Case Concerning Rights of Nationals of the United States of America in Morocco, Judgement ICJ Rep. (1952).
19. Fisheries Case, Judgement ICJ Rep. (1951).
20. R. Y. Jennings, "The Identification and Identity of International Law," in International Law: Teaching and Practice, ed. B. Cheng (London: Stevens & Sons, 1982), 6.
21. North Sea Continental Shelf Cases, Judgement ICJ Rep. (Dissenting Opinion Judge Lachs) (1969).
22. I. Brownlie, Principles of Public International Law, 3rd ed. (Oxford: Clarendon Press, 1966), 8.
23. Committee on Formation of Customary (General) International Law, Final Report of the Committee, Statement of Principles Applicable to the Formation

of General Customary International Law, International Law Association, London Conference 27 n. 68 (2000).

24. J. Green, The Persistent Objector Rule in International Law (Oxford: Hart Publishing, 2016), 1 (citing C. van Bynkershoek, De Foro Legatorum Liber Singularis: A Monograph on the Jurisdiction over Ambassadors in Both Civil and Criminal Cases (1721), 106-07).
25. Ibid., 25.
26. J. Green (citing Emer de Vattel, The Law of Nations, or Principles of the Law of Nature Applied to the Conduct and Affairs of Nations and Sovereigns, ed. Joseph Chitty, 6th ed. (Philadelphia: T. & J.W. Johnson, 1844), 1xv, ¶ 26 (1758).
27. Ibid., 25-26 (citing G.F. von Martens, A Compendium of the Law of Nations, Founded on the Treaties and Customs of the Modern Nations of Europe, trans. W. Cobbett (London: G.G. and J. Robinson, 1802), 356 (1788).
28. Ibid., 25-26.
29. Ibid., 26.
30. T. Helfman, "The Court of Vice Admiralty at Sierra Leone and the Abolition of the West African Slave Trade," Yale Law Journal 115 (2006): 1122, 1150-51.
31. J. Dodson, A Report of the Case of the Louis, Forest, Master, 1817, Appealed from the Vice Admiralty Court at Sierra Leone, and Determined in the High Court of Admiralty (London: J. Butterworth, 1817), 48-52.
32. The Antelope, 23 U.S. 66 (1825).
33. M. H. Mendelson, The Formation of Customary International Law (Oxford: Clarendon Press, 1998), 232-33.
34. The Antelope, 23 U.S. 66 (1825).
35. The Paquete Habana, 175 U.S. 677, 700 (1900).
36. C. Bradley and M. Gulati, "Withdrawing from International Custom," Yale Law Journal 120 (2010): 202, 213.
37. Fischbach and Friedericy Cases, (Germany v. Venezuelan), 10 RIAA 357 (Mixed Claim Comm. 1903).
38. Ibid.
39. Ibid.
40. Ibid.

The Persistent Objector and Original Consent

1. J. Gifford, "Jus Cogens and the Fourteenth Amendment Privileges or Immunities: Framework of Substantive Fundamental Human Rights in a

Constitutional Safe Harbor," Arizona Journal of International & Comparative Law 16 (1999): 481.

2. C. Bradley, "The Juvenile Death Penalty and International Law," Duke Law Journal 52 (2002): 485, 516-35.
3. The United States' consent to the principle of universalism can be deduced from its language and action throughout the past half century. P. Curran, "Universalism, Relativism, and Private Enforcement of Customary International Law," Chicago Journal of International Law 5 (2004): 311.
4. Statute of the International Court of Justice, 59 Stat 1055, TS No. 933, art. 38.
5. A. D'Amato, "The Concept of Human Rights in International Law," Columbia Law Review 82 (1982): 1110, 1127.
6. Reducing the power of treaty reservations and the effects it has on States' decisions to commit to a given treaty can be problematic. States are not immune to the pressure or coercive actions that other States can bring. See O. Hathaway, "Between Power and Principle: An Integrated Theory of International Law," University of Chicago Law Review 72 (2005): 469.
7. I. Brownlie, Principles of Public International Law, 6th ed. (Oxford: Oxford University Press, 1990); M. Villiger, Customary International Law and Treaties (Dordrecht: Martinus Nijhoff, 1985), 15-17.
8. Fisheries Case, Judgement ICJ Rep. (1951).
9. Ibid.
10. Ibid.
11. Colombian-Peruvian Asylum Case, Judgment ICJ Rep. (1950).
12. A. D'Amato, The Concept of Custom in International Law (Ithaca: Cornell University Press, 1971), 88-89; G.H. Van Hoof, Rethinking the Sources of International Law (Deventer: Kluwer, 1983), 107-108.
13. P. Dumberry, "The Last Citadel! Can a State Claim the Status of Persistent Objector to Prevent the Application of a Rule of Customary International Law in Investor-State Arbitration?" Leiden Journal of International Law 23 (2010): 379, 387.
14. Ibid.
15. Ibid.
16. H. Lau, "Rethinking the Persistent Objector Doctrine in International Human Rights Law," Chicago Journal of International Law 6 (2005): 500.
17. United Nations Conference on the Law of Treaties, Official Records, First Session, Meetings of the Committee of the Whole (Vienna: United Nations, 1969), 309-310, 388.
18. Ibid.

19. United Nations Security Council Official Records, 29th Year, 1800th Meeting (New York: United Nations, 1974), 11, 15.
20. See the Barcelona Traction, Light, and Power Company Ltd Case, Judgement ICJ Rep. (1970); The US Diplomatic and Consular Case, Judgement ICJ Rep. (1980).
21. The Fisheries Case, Pleadings ICJ Rep.
22. J. Charney, "The Persistent Objector Rule and the Development of Customary International Law," British Yearbook of International Law 12 (1985): 12-14.
23. S. Rosenne, Practice and Methods of International Law (Dordrecht: Martinus Nijhoff, 1984), 66.
24. G. Danilenko, "The Theory of International Customary Law," German Yearbook of International Law 31 (1988): 43.
25. Charney, "The Persistent Objector Rule," 16-19.
26. T. Stein, "The Approach of the Different Drummer: The Principle of the Persistent Objector in International Law," Harvard International Law Journal 26 (1985): 477-478.
27. Island of Palmas Case (or Miangas) (United States v. Netherlands) Award (1928) II RIAA 829, ICGJ 392 (PCA 1928).
28. The Namibia and Fisheries Jurisdiction cases are representative of this. In the Tunisia/Libya Continental Shelf case, the Compromis of Arbitration encompassed, as part of the applicable law, the "new trends" in the Third UN Conference on the Law of the Sea. Counsel for Tunisia explained that the parties intended, by that provision, to 'reinterpret the existing rules in light of these new trends in order to remain in step with the evolution of the law'. Continental Shelf Case (Tunisia v. Libya), ICJ Pleadings.

Chapter V: The Subjective Element

1. E. Kadens and E. Young, "How Customary is Customary International Law?" William & Mary Law Review 54 (2013): 885, 907.
2. See Military and Paramilitary Activities in and against Nicaragua Case, Merits, Judgement, ICJ Rep. (1986).
3. Case Concerning Right of Passage over Indian Territory, Judgement, ICJ (1960).
4. Ibid.
5. Ibid.
6. See Colombian-Peruvian Asylum Case, Judgement, ICJ Rep. (1950).
7. See Case Concerning Rights of Nationals of the United States of America in Morocco, Judgement, ICJ (1952).
8. North Sea Continental Shelf Cases, Judgement, ICJ Rep. (1969).

9. See The SS Lotus Case, Judgment, PCIJ (1927).
10. See Military and Paramilitary activities in and against Nicaragua Case, Merits, Judgement, ICJ (1986).
11. Ibid.
12. Ibid.
13. Ibid.
14. Ibid.
15. Ibid.
16. See Nottebohm Case, Judgement, ICJ Rep. (1955).
17. See The SS Lotus Case (1927).
18. See Military and Paramilitary Case (1986).
19. The Fisheries Jurisdiction (United Kingdom v. Iceland), Merits, Judgement ICJ Rep. (1974).
20. The Right of Passage Case, (1960).
21. The Lotus Case, (1927).
22. See Case Concerning United States Diplomatic and Consular Staff in Tehran, Judgement, ICJ Rep. (1980).
23. The Fisheries Jurisdiction Case, (1974).
24. See Reservation to Genocide Convention, Opinion, ICJ Rep. (1951).
25. H. Kelsen, General Theory of Law and State (Cambridge, MA: Harvard University Press, 1945), 78.
26. H. Kelsen, General Theory of Norms (Oxford: Clarendon Press, 1991), 136.
27. L. Lloyd of Hampstead and M. Freeman, Lloyd's Introduction to Jurisprudence, 5th ed. (London: Stevens & Sons, 1985), 445.
28. A. White, Rights (Oxford: Clarendon Press, 1984), 55-73.
29. R. Dworkin, Taking Rights Seriously (Cambridge, MA: Harvard University Press, 1977), 22-31.
30. See, inter alia, M. Shaw, International Law, 3rd ed. (Cambridge: Cambridge University Press, 1991), 72; This notion has been brought up by States during their appearance before the Court. See Case Concerning Right of Passage Over India Territory, ICJ Pleadings.
31. H.L.A. Hart, The Concept of Law, 2nd ed. (Oxford: Oxford University Press, 1991), 83.
32. I. MacGibbon, "Customary International Law and Acquiescence," British Yearbook of International Law 33 (1957): 125-126.
33. Ibid.
34. H. Kelsen, General Theory of Law and State (Cambridge, MA: Harvard University Press, 1945), 59.

35. Ibid.
36. P. Guggenheim, Traité de Droit International Public, Tome I (Geneva: Georg, 1953), 46-48.
37. Ibid (Translation by author).
38. H. Kelsen, Principles of International Law (New York: Rinehart, 1952), 20-25.
39. H.L.A. Hart, The Concept of Law, 2nd ed. (Oxford: Oxford University Press, 1991), 84-85.
40. Ibid.
41. Ibid.
42. Ibid.
43. Ibid.
44. Kelsen, General Theory of Law and State, 72-74.
45. Ibid.
46. Ibid.
47. Hart, The Concept of Law, 56.
48. Ibid.
49. O. Schachter, "Toward a Theory of International Obligation," in The Effectiveness of International Decisions, ed. S. Schwebel (Dobbs Ferry, NY: Oceana Publications, 1971), 9-31.
50. R. Ago, "Positive Law and International Law," American Journal of International Law 51 (1957): 700-701.
51. Right of Passage Case, Judgement ICJ Rep. (1960).
52. Ibid.
53. O. Schachter, "Towards a Theory of International Obligation," 21.
54. North Seas Cases, ICJ Pleadings (Federal Republic of Germany); Fisheries Case, ICJ Pleading (United Kingdom).
55. For a more detailed examination of this see M. Koskenniemi, From Apology to Utopia (Cambridge: Cambridge University Press, 1989), 340-421.
56. P. Reuter, Introduction to the Law of Treaties (London: Pinter Publishers, 1989), 110.
57. M.H. Mendelson, "State Acts and Omissions as Explicit or Implicit Claims," in Le droit International au service de la paix, de la justice et du development (Paris: Pedone, 1991), 379-381.
58. Yearbook of the International Law Commission, vol. I (New York: United Nations, 1950), 4-7.

Evolutionary Developments in Customary International Law

1. B. Cheng, "Custom: The Future of General State Practice in a Divided World," in The Structure and Process of International Law, ed. R. Macdonald and D. Johnston (Dordrecht: Martinus Nijhoff, 1983), 513-554.
2. Ibid.
3. Ibid.
4. Ibid.
5. Ibid.
6. Ibid., 536-537.
7. North Sea Continental Shelf Cases, ICJ Rep. (1969).
8. Cheng, "Custom: The Future of General State Practice," 538.
9. Ibid., 537.
10. Ibid., 539.
11. Ibid., 538.
12. Ibid., 523.
13. Ibid., 534.
14. Ibid., 531-32.
15. Ibid., 537.
16. A. D'Amato, The Concept of Custom in International Law (Ithaca: Cornell University Press, 1971), 18, 86.
17. Ibid., 76.
18. Ibid., 88.
19. Ibid.
20. Ibid.
21. G. Del Vecchio, The Formal Bases of Law (Boston: Boston Book Company, 1921), 101.
22. K. Popper, The Logic of Scientific Discovery (New York: Basic Books, 1959), 27-48.
23. O. Schachter, "The Nature and Process of Legal Development in International Society," in The Structure and Process of International Law, ed. R. MacDonald and D. Johnston (Dordrecht: Martinus Nijhoff, 1983), 756-757; W. Twining and D. Miers, How to Do Things with Rules, 3rd ed. (London: Weidenfeld and Nicolson, 1991), 131.
24. H. Thirlway, International Customary Law and Codification (Leiden: A.W. Sijthoff, 1972), 55.
25. Ibid., 55-56.

26. J. Scott, ed., "Selection from the Works of Francisco Suarez," in The Classics of International Law, vol. II (Oxford: Clarendon Press, 1944), 565-566.
27. C. Rousseau, Droit International Public (Paris: Sirey, 1970), 323.
28. See North Sea Cases, Diss. Opinion of Judge Tanaka and Judge Koretsky.
29. Del Vecchio, The Formal Bases of Law, 214-217.
30. Case Concerning Right of Passage over Indian Territory, Pleadings, ICJ Rep.
31. Ibid.
32. Ibid.
33. Yearbook of the International Law Commission, vol. I (New York: United Nations, 1950), 6-7.
34. H. Lauterpacht, International Law (Cambridge: Cambridge University Press, 1970), 63-64.

The Relationship between the Subjective Element and State Practice

1. C. de Visscher, Theories et realites en droit international public (Paris: Pedone, 1953); G. Gregoire, La coutume en droit international (Brussels: Bruylant, 1931), 132-133.
2. P. Reuter, Droit international public (Paris: Presses universitaires de France, 1976), 94.
3. R. Ihering, Law as a Means to an End (Boston: Boston Book Company, 1924), 9.
4. The creation, in 1958, of a Committee on the Peaceful Uses of the Outer Space with a view to, inter alia, elaborating a study on the legal questions arising out of the exploration of outer space seems to endorse Situation B. UN General Assembly Resolution 1348 (XIII), UN Doc. A/C.1/L.220/REV.1, Yearbook of the United Nations (New York: United Nations, 1959), 24-29.
5. Permitted means that the practice or action is not juridically prohibited. A permissive practice engenders a situation where international law is unsettled.
6. Platzoder and Vitzthum, Seerecht, Law of the Sea (Berlin: Duncker & Humblot, 1984), 477-478.
7. For instance, this was the conclusion reached by the Joint Separate Opinion of Judges Forester, Bengzon, Arechaga, Singh, and Ruda in the Fisheries Jurisdiction case, with regard to fishery limits in international law. Fisheries Jurisdiction (United Kingdom v. Iceland), Merits, Judgement, ICJ Rep. (1974).
8. This is similar to when a State settles a question by means of an ex gratia payment, refusing to admit the contentions of the other party.

Chapter VI: The Customary Process: A Theoretical and Practical Examination

State Actions and the International System

1. Z. Mapz, National Choice and International Processes (Princeton: Princeton University Press, 1990), 4.
2. R. Cohen, International Politics, 2nd ed. (Englewood Cliffs, NJ: Prentice Hall, 1986), 14-18.
3. E. Luard, International Society (New York: New Amsterdam Books, 1990), 61-63.

State Preferences and Interactions in International Relations

1. The Declaration of Colonial Rights (1774).
2. Ibid.
3. United States Const. art. I, § 8, cl. 3.
4. Security Council Official Records, Doc. S/14976, Thirty-Seventh Year (New York: United Nations, 1982), 21-22.
5. R. Axelrod, "An Evolutionary Approach to Norms," American Political Science Review 80 (1986): 1095-1098.
6. Ibid.
7. K. Simmonds, "New Directions in the Law of the Sea," Ch. 12, in New Directions in the Law of the Sea (Dobbs Ferry, NY: Oceana Publications, 1992), 1.

State Acts and Legal Relationships

1. A. White, Rights (Oxford: Clarendon Press, 1984), 121-124.
2. Ibid., 116-120.
3. M. Whiteman, Digest of International Law, vol. IV (Washington, DC: U.S. Department of State, 1965), 114.
4. It is perhaps in light of those criteria that one should determine in a given case which are the States "whose interests are specially affected". The Court in the North Sea Continental Shelf case used this phrase. North Continental Shelf Case, ICJ Rep. (1969).
5. M.H. Mendelson, "State Acts and Omissions as Explicit or Implicit Claims," in Le droit international au service de la paix, de la justice et du developpement, Melanges en honneur de Michel Virally (Paris: Pedone, 1991), 379.
6. Office of the Federal Register, "Proclamation 2668- Policy of the United States with Respect to Coastal Fisheries in Certain Areas of the High Seas" (Washington, DC: National Archives, 1945).

7. See Delimitation of the Maritime Boundary in the Gulf of Maine Area, Judgement, ICJ Rep. (1984); Frontier Dispute, Judgement, ICJ Rep. (Sep. Op. of Judge Luchaire) (1986).
8. See Case Concerning the Temple of Vihear (Cambodia v. Thailand), Merits, Judgement, ICJ Rep. (1962).
9. Fisheries Case, Judgement, ICJ Rep. (1951); See also Affaires des Gribadarna (Norway v. Sweden), UN Reports of International Arbitral Awards, vol. XI (New York: United Nations), 161.
10. See Case Concerning Right of Passage Over Indian Territory, Judgement, ICJ Rep. (Diss. Opin. Of Judge Armand-Ugon) (1960).
11. See Land, Island and Maritime Frontier Dispute (El Salvador/Honduras: Nicaragua Intervening), Judgement ICJ Rep. (1992).
12. Ibid.
13. See Temple of Vihear Case (Cambodia v. Thailand), Judgement ICJ Rep. (Sep. Opin. Of Sir Gerald Fitzmaurice) (1962).
14. D. Bowett, "Estoppel Before International Tribunals and Its Relationship to Acquiescence," British Yearbook of International Law 33 (1957): 201-202.
15. See Nuclear Tests Case (Australia v. France), Judgement, ICJ Rep. (1974).
16. H. Lauterpacht, "Sovereignty Over Submarine Areas," British Yearbook of International Law 27 (1950): 396.

Positive Acts, Recognition, and Renunciation

1. This instance was cited by the Joint Separate Opinion of Judges Foster, Bengzon, Arehaga, Singh and Rucha in the Fisheries Jurisdiction case (United Kingdom v. Iceland) (1974).
2. M. Whiteman, Digest of International Law, vol. VI (Washington, DC: U.S. Department of State, 1965), 115.
3. Office of the Special Representative of the Secretary-General for the Law of the Sea, The Law of the Sea (New York: United Nations, 1987), 138.
4. Ibid.
5. Judge Lachs suggests, in the North Sea cases, that one of the ways in which a customary process is started is by States adopting "unilateral acts relying on the confident expectation that they will find acquiescence or be emulated". North Sea Continental Shelf Cases, ICJ Rep. (1969).
6. A. Szekeley, Latin America and the Development of the Law of the Sea (London: Frances Pinter, 1986), 13-16; For the text of the U.S. complaint see UN Legislative Series, Laws and Regulations on the Regime of the High Seas, ST/LEG/SER.B/1 (New York: United Nations, 1951), 6-8.

7. Whiteman, Digest of International Law, 796.
8. Platzoder and Vitzthum, Seerecht, Law of the Sea, 479-480.
9. Churchill et al., New Directions in the Law of the Sea (Dobbs Ferry, NY: Oceana Publications, 1977), 12-13.
10. K. Simmonds, New Directions in the Law of the Sea, vol. 3 (Dobbs Ferry, NY: Oceana Publications, 1992), 5.
11. See Land, Island, and Maritime Frontier Dispute (El Salvador/Honduras: Nicaragua Intervening), Judgement, ICJ Rep. (1992).
12. Ibid.
13. See Fisheries Jurisdiction Case (United Kingdom v. Iceland), Judgement, ICJ Rep. (Diss. Op. of Judge Gros) (1974).
14. The Minquiers and Ecrehos Case, Judgement ICJ Rep. (Indiv. Opin. Of Judge Levi Carneiro) (1953).
15. Ibid.
16. Ibid.
17. See the fisheries dispute that arose between the Solomon Islands and the United States, Tsamenyi, M. "The Jeannette Diana Dispute," Ocean Development and International Law 16 (1986): 356-367.
18. See Brazil and the United States of America, Agreement Concerning Shrimp, 35-39 UNTS, vol. 894 (New York: United Nations, 1973).
19. A. Castro and L. Augusto, O Brasil e o Novo Direito do Mar (Rio de Janeiro: Forense, 1989), 27. (Trans. By the author).
20. Declarations by the United Kingdom Representative in the United Nations, Doc. A/42/PV.70, 38; and Doc. A/AC.109/PV.1223, 32.

Effects of the General State of the Law

1. Platzoder and Vitzthum, Seerecht, Law of the Sea, 477.

The Codification and Development of International Law

1. See Review of the Multilateral Treaty-Making Process, Doc. ST/LEG/SER.B/21 (New York: United Nations, 1985), 7-38.
2. Statute of the International Law Commission, arts. 16(c), (h), (j), 19(2), 20, 21(2), 22 (1947).
3. I. Sinclair, "The Impact of the Unratified Codification Convention," in Realism in Law-Making, ed. A. Bos and H. Siblesz (Dordrecht: Martinus Nijhoff, 1986), 228.

4. See R. Ago, "Nouvelles reflexions sur la codification du droit international," in International Law at a Time of Perplexity, ed. Y. Dinstein (Dordrecht: Martinus Nijhoff, 1989), 8-9.
5. A good example of a UN General Assembly resolution performing the function of a follow-up mechanism is UN Res. 40/73 of 11 December 1985, on the "consideration of effective measures to enhance the protection, security and safety of diplomatic and consular missions and representatives." This resolution urged all States to observe and implement principles and rules of international law governing diplomatic and consular relations and requested, inter alia, that all States report violations to the Secretary-General.
6. J. Arechaga, "Customary International Law and the Conference on the Law of the Sea," in Essays in International Law in Honor of Judge Manfred Lachs, ed. J. Makarczyk (The Hague: Martinus Nijhoff, 1984), 576-585; H. Caaminos and V. Marotta-Rangel, "The Sources of the Law of the Sea," in A Handbook on the New Law of the Sea, ed. R. Dupuy et al. (Dordrecht: Martinus Nijhoff, 1991), 77-81.

Chapter VII: The Development of Customary International Law and the Two-Hundred-Mile EEZ

1. For instance, Hans Kelsen states that "custom by which a norm of general international law is created" is a "long established practice of state." H. Kelsen, Principles of International Law (New York: Rinehart, 1952), 445; Bing Cheng commented, "not only it unnecessary that the usage should be prolonged but there need also be no usage at all in the sense of repeated practice, provided that opinio juris of the states concerned can be clearly established. Consequently, international customary law has in reality only one constitutive element, the opinio juris. Where there is opinio juris, there is a rule of customary international law." B. Cheng, "United Nations Resolutions on Outer Space 'Instant' International Customary Law," Indian Journal of International Law 5 (1965): 106-7.
2. See M. O. Hudson, "Article 24 of the Statute of the International Law Commission," Yearbook of the International Law Commission 2, UN Doc. A/CN.4/16/Add.1 (New York: United Nations, 1950), 5.
3. This element is also identified by the ICJ Asylum Case (Colombia v. Peru), ICJ Rep. (1950): 266; and the Anglo-Norwegian Fisheries Case (United Kingdom v. Norway), ICJ Rep. 116 (1951).
4. This element is noted in the North Sea Continental Shelf Cases (1969), 74.
5. In the Lotus Case, the Permanent Court noted that, in determining the motivation of a state abstaining from action, "only if such abstentions were based on their being conscious of a duty to abstain would it be

possible to speak of an international custom," Case of the S. S. Lotus (France v. Turkey), PCIJ, Series A. No. 10 (Sept. 7, 1927), 28; see also North Sea Continental Shelf Cases (1969), 41-44.

6. See Temple of Preah Vihear Case, (Cambodia v. Thailand), ICJ Rep. 25-27 and 29-30 (1962).
7. North Sea Continental Shelf Cases (1969), 42-43.
8. Ibid., 227.
9. J. D'Arechaga, Case Concerning the Continental Shelf (Tunisia v. Libyan Arab Jamahiriya), ICJ Rep. 115 para. 54 (1982).
10. J. L. Kunz, "The Nature of Customary International Law," American Journal of International Law 47 (1953): 662, 666.
11. P. E. Corbett, "The Consent of States and the Sources of the Law of Nations," British Yearbook of International Law 6 (1925): 20, 24-25.
12. G. I. Tunkin, Theory of International Law (Cambridge, MA: Harvard University Press, 1974), 124.
13. In the Anglo-Norwegian Fisheries Case, the ICJ observed that it is not necessary for the customary norm to pass the test of "universal acceptance."
14. I. Brownlie, Principles of Public International Law, 6th ed. (Oxford: Oxford University Press, 1990), 6-7.
15. Asylum Case (Colombia v. Peru) (1950), 276. The Court reaffirmed this view in Rights of Nationals of the United States in Morocco Case (United States v. France), ICJ Rep. 200 (1952).
16. H. Lauterpacht, The Development of International Law by the International Court (Cambridge: Cambridge University Press, 2011), 378. The Court referred to "consistent international practice" in the Wimbledon Case (France, Italy, Japan, and the United Kingdom v. Germany), PCIJ Ser. A, No. 1 (Aug. 17, 1923), 26-28.
17. Asylum Case (Colombia v. Peru) (1950), 15.
18. Case Concerning Military and Paramilitary Activities in and Against Nicaragua (Nicaragua v. United States), Merits, ICJ Rep. 14 (1986); also, Anglo-Norwegian Fisheries Case, ICJ Rep. 128 (1951).
19. Case Concerning Military and Paramilitary Activities (1986).
20. D. Johnson and E. Gold, "Extended Jurisdiction: The Impact of UNCLOS III on Coastal State Practice," in The Law of the Sea: State Practice in Zones of Special Jurisdiction, Proceedings of the Thirteen Annual Conference October 15-18, ed. T. A. Clingan (Honolulu: Law of the Sea Institute, 1979), 27-49.
21. Ibid.

22. L. Lee, "The Law of the Sea Convention and Third States," American Journal of International Law 77 (1983): 541-568.
23. A. J. Zakharov, "Comment to Article by C. A. Fleischer, the Exclusive Economic Zone under the Convention Regime and in State Practice," in The 1982 Convention on the Law of the Sea, Proceedings of the Seventeenth Annual Conference, July 12-16, 1983, ed. A. Koers and B. Oxman (Honolulu: Law of the Sea Institute, 1984), 364; also, the comments of I. Kolosovski, in The 1982 Convention on the Law of the Sea, Proceedings of the Seventeenth Annual Conference, July 12-16, 1983, ed. A. Koers and B. Oxman (Honolulu: Law of the Sea Institute, 1984), 367; A. Kolodkin and A. Zakharov, "Some Aspects of Soviet State Practice on the Development of Ocean Resources," in Consensus and Confrontation: The United States and the Law of the Sea Convention, ed. J. M. Van Dyke (Honolulu: Law of the Sea Institute, 1985), 214.
24. P. Sreenivasa Rao, "Public Order of Oceans: Problems and Prospects," Indian Journal of International Law 17 (1977): 232.
25. Act Concerning the Maritime Areas of the Polish Republic and the Maritime Administration, 1991, Law of the Sea Bulletin 21 (1991): 66.
26. Ibid.
27. Ibid.
28. Sweden's Act on Sweden's Economic Zone (December 3, 1992); see also S. Mahmoudi, "Sweden's Economic Zone Act," International Journal of Marine and Coastal Law 28 (1993): 524.
29. S. Kaye and D. Rothwell, "Australia's Antarctic Maritime Claims and Boundaries," Ocean Development and International Law 26, no. 3 (1995): 209.
30. B. Kwiatkowska, "Exclusive Economic Zone: General Evaluation," in Essays on the New Law of the Sea, ed. B. Vukas (Zagreb: Sveučilište u Zagrebu, 1985), 110.
31. See M. Lazarev, "The Sea Economic Zone: An Important Problem of the 'Package'," Indian Journal of International Law 17 (1977): 209-215.
32. See, for example, Zakharov, "Comment to Article by C. A. Fleischer," 364; Kolosovski, The 1982 Convention on the Law of the Sea, Ibid.
33. Takeo Iguchi, "The Law of the Sea: Conventional Rules and Customary Norms," paper presented at the Annual Meeting of the American Society of International Law, Boston, MA, April 9, 1987 (mimeograph), 5.
34. Ibid., 5-6.
35. For the views of Eastern European authors, see comments by J. Symonides, "The Concept and Claims of Geographically Disadvantaged States at the Third United Nations Law of the Sea Conference," in The Management of Humanity's Resources: The Law of the Sea Workshop, The Hague, 29-31

Oct. 1981, ed. R. Dupuy (The Hague: Martinus Nijhoff, 1982), 298. For those writers from developing states, see R. Anand, "The Politics of a New Legal Order for Fisheries," Ocean Development and International Law 11 (1982): 280, 282-83. For the views expressed by Western authors, see A. Koers, "The United Nations Convention on the Law of the Sea: An Overview," in The International Law of the Sea, Issues of Implementation in Indonesia, Proceedings of a Seminar at Jakarta on 22-27 August, 1983, ed. E. Hey and A. Koers (Jakarta: Indonesian Institute of Sciences, 1984), 23-25; L. Lee, "The Law of the Sea Convention and Third States," American Journal of International Law 77 (1983): 566-567; James L. Malone, "Freedom and Opportunity: Foundation for a Dynamic Ocean Policy," Department of State Bulletin 84, no. 2093 (1984): 77.

36. Ibid., 76-79.; Lee, "The Law of the Sea Convention and Third States" (1983).
37. Lee, "The Law of the Sea Convention and Third States," 568 (1983); also Koers, "The United Nations Convention on the Law of the Sea," 23 (1984); Guy de Lacharrière, "La Reforme du Droit de la Mer et le Rôle de la Conférence des Nations Unies," in Le Nouveau Droit International de la Mer, ed. D. Bardonnet and M. Virally (Paris: Editions A. Pédone, 1983), 27-32.
38. Case Concerning Delimitation of the Maritime Boundary in the Gulf of Maine Area (Canada v. United States), ICJ Rep. 299-300 (1984).
39. B. Kwiatkowska, "New Soviet Legislation on the 200-Mile Economic Zone and Certain Problems of Evolution of Customary Law," Netherlands International Law Review 33 (1986): 43.

Repetition of the Practice over a Considerable Time Period

1. H. Kelsen, Principles of International Law (New York: Rinehart, 1952), 445.
2. B. Lepard, Customary International Law: A New Theory with Practical Applications (Cambridge: Cambridge University Press, 2010), 122-139.
3. Opinion of B. Cheng, Kelsen, Principles of International Law.
4. R. R. Baxter, "Treaties and Custom," Recueil des Cours de l'Académie de Droit International 129 (1970): 61-62.
5. D'Arechaga, "Case Concerning the Continental Shelf," 228 para. 120.
6. "International legal doctrine of other countries, with rare exceptions, considers, recognition or opinio juris a necessary and decisive element for the creation of a customary norm of international law." Tunkin, Theory of International Law, 119.
7. C. Hudson, "Fishery and Economic Zones as Customary International Law," South Dakota Law Review 17, no. 3 (1980): 661-689.

8. W. Extavour, The Exclusive Economic Zone: A Study of the Evolution and Progressive Development of International Law of the Sea (Geneva: Institut universitaire de hautes études internationales, 1979), 171-176.
9. See "Convention Relative au Développement Régional des Pêches dans le Golf de Guinee," Revue Generale de Droit International Public 91 (1987): 1115; "Preamble to the Niue Treaty on Cooperation in Fisheries Surveillance and Law Enforcement in the South Pacific Region, June 9, 1992," International Legal Materials 32 (1993): 136; also "Procureur de la République v. J. Crujeiras Tome, 1981," Revue Generale de Droit International Public (1983): 465.
10. Attard, The Exclusive Economic Zone in International Law, 19.
11. I. C. MacGibbon, "The Scope of Acquiescence in International Law," British Yearbook of International Law 31 (1954): 143.
12. The dissenting state can also show its dissent by means of an express statement or vote against a particular rule. See Mark E. Villiger, Customary International Law and Treaties: A Study of Their Interactions and Interrelations, with Special Considerations of the 1969 Vienna Convention on the Law of Treaties (Dordrecht: Martinus Nijhoff, 1985), 15.
13. It must be acknowledged that the declaration referred to the development of the two-hundred-mile EEZ that were set forth in the preambular clauses. These considerations included a need to reinforce the principle of coastal state sovereignty over natural resources, supported by the OAU and the UN General Assembly in various resolutions; the right of African countries to exploit the resources of the sea surrounding their continent for the benefit of their peoples; the nonparticipation of African states at UNCLOS I and UNCLOS II; and the imbalance between the developed and developing states in their capacity to access and enjoy the resources of the sea. Judge Dillard also emphasized the absence of protests against assertions that did not exceed 12 miles, ibid., 58.
14. See "Temple of Preah Vihear Case, (Cambodia v. Thailand)," ICJ Rep. (1962): 25-27 and 29-30.
15. Ibid., 29.
16. For the text of the Fishery Conservation and Management Act, see International Legal Materials 15 (1976): 635.
17. Law No. 1-81 of 181, in the Act of February 10, 1976 Regulating the Provisions of Paragraph 8 of Article 27 of the Political Constitution of the United Mexican States Concerning the Exclusive Economic Zone.
18. L. D. M. Nelson, "The Emerging New Law of the Sea," Modern Law Review 42 (1979): 54.

19. For example, D'Arechaga, "Case Concerning the Continental Shelf," 70 para. 100; "Case Concerning Delimitation of the Maritime Boundary in the Gulf of Maine Area," 265, para. 19; "Case Concerning the Delimitation of Marine Areas between Canada and the French Republic," International Legal Materials 31, no. 1145 (1992): 175, para. 88.
20. See Robert Y. Jennings, "What Is International Law, and How Do We Tell It When We See it," Swiss Yearbook of International Law 37 (1981): 82; Charney, "The Exclusive Economic Zone and Public International Law," 283-85.
21. T. Iguchi, "The Law of the Sea: Conventional Rules and Customary Norms." Paper presented at the Annual Meeting of the American Society of International Law, Boston, MA, April 9, 1987 (mimeograph).
22. A. Kolodkin and A. Zakharov, "Some Aspects of Soviet State Practice on the Development of Ocean Resources." In Consensus and Confrontation: The United States and the Law of the Sea Convention, edited by John M. Van Dyke. Honolulu: Law of the Sea Institute, University of Hawaii, 1985: 214.

The Scope of the EEZ Concept in Customary International Law

1. See Michael Akehurst, A Modern Introduction to International Law (London: Routledge, 1982), 270-72; Jesper Grolin, "The Future of the Law of the Sea: Consequences of a Non Treaty or Non-Universal Treaty Situation," Ocean Development and International Law 13 (1983): 8-9.
2. Fleischer, "The Exclusive Economic Zone under the Convention Regime and in State Practice," 250.
3. See UN Division for Ocean Affairs and the Law of the Sea. Practice of States, 10.
4. It is noteworthy that, in practical terms, several EFZ claimant states exercise some type of jurisdiction over MSR in their own EFZs. See, for instance, Note from the Permanent Mission of Japan to the United Nations on Provisional Procedures for a Request to Conduct Marine Scientific Research by Foreign Research Vessels in the Territorial Sea, on the Continental Shelf or in the Fishing Zone of Japan, 28 July 1988, in UN Division for Ocean Affairs and the Law of the Sea, The Law of the Sea, 143; and Note to the United Nations on Regulations Governing Scientific Research in Waters under Belgian Jurisdiction, November 1, 1988, in ibid., 33. For additional details, also see Soons, "Regulation of Marine Scientific Research," 267-71.
5. Smith, Exclusive Economic Zone Claims, 34.
6. Ibid., 38.
7. Ibid., 35-37 Table 7.

8. Vicuña, The Exclusive Economic Zone, 149.
9. See UN Division for Ocean Affairs and the Law of the Sea. Practice of States, 14.
10. "Convention on the Continental Shelf."
11. "The Law of the Sea Convention."
12. Of the thirty states that are not party to the LOS Convention, fifteen are coastal states and fifteen are landlocked states. The coastal states that are not a party to the convention include Colombia, Iran, Israel, Peru, Turkey, the United States, and Venezuela. The number of states party to the 1958 Geneva Convention on the LOS is relatively small: Convention on the Territorial Sea and the Contiguous Zone, 52 parties; Convention on the Continental Shelf, 58 parties; and Convention on the High Seas, 63 parties, "Convention on the Continental Shelf."
13. Examples include Articles 16 of the Agreement on Cooperation on Marine Oil Pollution Preparedness and Response in the Artic, 15 May 2013; Article 16 of the International Convention for the Control and Management of Ships' Ballast Water and Sediments, 2004, 13 February 2004; and Article 15 of the International Convention on the Control of Harmful Anti-Fouling Systems on Ships, 2001, October 5, 2001.
14. Decisions of institutions that are created by the LOS Convention, supra note 72, such as the International Tribunal for the Law of the Sea (ITLOS), and Annexes VII and VIII arbitral tribunals are not likely to address the first question since only parties to the Convention may invoke their jurisdictional powers. However, Article 293(1) of the LOS Convention requires tribunals to apply "other rules of international law not incompatible with" the LOS convention where the convention did not refer to those rules.
15. United States, "President's Ocean Policy Statement, March 10, 1983," The Division of Ocean Affairs and the Law of the Sea.
16. Joint Statement by the United States and Soviet Union, with Uniform Interpretation of Rules of International Law Governing Innocent Passage. September 2, 1989. Law of the Sea Bulletin 14 (1989): 12-13; International Legal Materials 28 (1989): 1444-47; and American Journal of International Law 84 (1990): 239-42.
17. International Law Association, "Final Report of the Committee on Formation of Customary (General) International Law: Statement of Principles Applicable to the Formation of General Customary International Law (as amended at the London Conference)," Report of the Sixty-Ninth Conference (London: International Law Association, 2000), 712-77.
18. International Law Commission (ILC), "Formation and Evidence of Customary International Law and Identification of Customary International Law." To

identify elements of the ILC's previous work on this issue, see UN Doc. A/CN.4/659 (March 14, 2013), and the Special Rapporteur's introductory Report, UN Doc. A/CN.4/663 (17 May 2013).

19. Yoshifumi Tanaka, The International Law of the Sea (Cambridge: Cambridge University Press, 2012), 12.
20. UN Doc. A/67/PV. 52 (December 12, 2012), 28. Venezuela objects to assertions of the universality of the LOS Convention for similar reasons, id., 27.
21. "Maritime Delimitation and Territorial Questions Between Qatar and Bahrain (Qatar v. Bahrain)," Judgment, ICJ Rep. (2001): 91, para. 167.
22. "Territorial and Maritime Dispute (Nicaragua v. Colombia)," Judgment, ICJ Rep. (2012): 666, para. 114.
23. "North Sea Continental Shelf Cases," 28-29, paras. 37-38, and 37-45, paras. 60-81.
24. See "Case Concerning Military and Paramilitary Activities in and Against Nicaragua," 97-98, paras. 184-86, for an examination of the Court's methodology in determining customary international rules. Churchill and Lowe, The Law of the Sea, 7, explain that "international custom" means "a general and consistent practice adopted by States," particularly the practice of states mostly directly concerned; and "evidence of a practice generally accepted as law, also known as opinio juris, means "the conviction that the practice is one which is either required or allowed by customary international law, or more generally that the practice concerns a matter which is the subject of legal regulation and is consistent with international law."

The Exclusive Economic Zone and Customary International Law

1. Case Concerning Delimitation of the Maritime Boundary in the Gulf of Maine Area, 294, para. 94.
2. "Case Concerning the Continental Shelf (Libyan Arab Jamahyria v. Malta)," 33, para. 34. "The institution of the exclusive economic zone, with its rule on entitlement by reason of distance, is shown by the practice of states to have become part of customary law."
3. Ibid.
4. "Case Concerning Military and Paramilitary Activities in and Against Nicaragua," 111, para. 214.
5. "Territorial and Maritime Dispute (Nicaragua v. Colombia)," 674, para. 139. The Court reaffirmed this conclusion in "Maritime Dispute (Peru v. Chile)," ICJ Rep. (2014): para. 179.

6. Views the U.S. expressed to the Republic of Korea in 2001 regarding USNS Bowditch, excerpted in Digest of U.S. Practice in International Law (Washington, DC: Government Printing Office, 2001), 698.
7. James Crawford, Brownlie's Principles of Public International Law, 8th ed. (Oxford: Oxford University Press, 2012), 265. Crawford states that "foreign ships have a right of innocent passage through the territorial sea in customary law"; Brownlie, Principles of Public International Law, 187, stated that the predecessor of Article 17 and 18 of the LOS Convention and article 14 of the Territorial Sea Convention, "in substance corresponds to the customary law, but it is more specific in certain respects."
8. Crawford, Brownlie's Principles of Public International Law, 297, referring to the Nicaragua v. United States Case.
9. Churchill and Lowe, The Law of the Sea, 161-62.
10. Ibid., 290. See also 291 for a discussion expressing doubts of a possible customary law rule requiring foreign fishing vessels be given access to any surplus in the EEZ.
11. Ibid., 409-10.
12. Crawford, Brownlie's Principles of Public International Law, 275-76.
13. United States Letter of Submittal on the Convention for the Conservation of Anadromous Stocks in the Northern Pacific, 14 May 1992, S. Treaty Doc. 102-30, excerpted in Digest of U.S. Practice in International Law, 1991-1999, 1703-4.
14. Tanaka, The International Law of the Sea, 385.

The High Seas

15. "Convention on the High Seas, Geneva."
16. Tanaka, The International Law of the Sea, 23. Concurred regarding Article 2.2.
17. Churchill and Lowe, The Law of the Sea, 204, stated that Articles 87 and 89 are customary international law. In a submission to the IMO's Marine Environment Protect Committee, the United States, Liberia, the Marshall Islands, Singapore, the International Association of Independent Tankers Owners, the International Chamber of Shipping, and the Oil Companies International Marine Forum stated: "The historical principles of the high seas freedoms of navigation are founded in customary international law and memorialized in Articles 58 and 87 of the United Nations Convention on the Law of the Sea, 1982 (UNCLOS)." IMO doc. MEPC 58/10/7, August 15, 2008, 2, para. 10.

18. Donald R. Rothwell and Tim Stephens, The International Law of the Sea (Oxford: Hart Publishing, 2010), 155. These authors noted that Article 89 "is consistent with customary international law on this matter."
19. Churchill and Lowe, The Law of the Sea, 258, expressed doubt that the genuine link requirement in Article 5(1) of the High Seas Convention represents customary international law.
20. Tanaka, The International Law of the Sea, 152 and 155 stated that the principle of the exclusive jurisdiction of the flag state (Article 92(1) first sentence) is well established in customary international law.
21. See the discussion of the travaux préparatoires of Article 10 of the High Seas Conventions, in Bernard Oxman, "The Duty to Respect Generally Accepted International Standards," New York University Journal of International Law and Politics 26 (1991): 109, 122-29.
22. Rothwell and Stephens, The International Law of the Sea, 161, surmised that Article 95, 96, and 236 "reflect existing customary international law with respect to sovereign immunity of states which itself is founded upon extensive jurisprudence by domestic courts and relevant municipal legislation."
23. Brownlie, Principles of Public International Law, 229, stated that the definition of piracy in Article 15 of the High Seas Convention is thought to represent the existing customary law. Tanaka, The International Law of the Sea, 160 noted, "[U]nder customary law and Article 105 of the LOSC, every State may seize a pirate ship or aircraft and arrest suspect pirate."
24. Churchill and Lowe, The Law of the Sea, 212, noted that Article 22 of the High Seas Convention and Article 110 of the LOS Convention "are generally regarded as codifying customary international law." Brownlie, Principles of Public International Law, believed that the right of approach in time of peace is recognized by customary law. Tanaka, The International Law of the Sea, 161, stated, "One can say that the right of visit to a ship that is engaged in the slave trade represents customary law."
25. Churchill and Lowe, The Law of the Sea, 214-15, acknowledged that the right of hot pursuit is recognized under customary international law.
26. Statement of the U.S. Representative to the UN Security Council, February 9, 1990, UN Doc. S/PV.2907 (February 9, 1990) 26-37, excerpted in Digest of U.S. Practice in International Law, 1989-1990, 454-55.
27. U.S. Department of State telegram to U.S. Embassy Muscat, December 6, 1989, excerpted in, ibid., 468-69.
28. "The M/V Saiga (No. 2) Case (St. Vincent and the Grenadian v. Guinea)," Judgment, (July 1, 1999).

29. James Crawford, Brownlie's Principles of International Law, 8th ed. (Oxford: Oxford University Press, 2012): 301.
30. Ibid., 303.
31. Ibid., 307.
32. Rothwell and Stephens, The International Law of the Sea, 77.
33. Crawford, Brownlie's Principles of International Law, 321.
34. "Case Concerning the Continental Shelf (Libyan Arab Jamahyria v. Malta)," 39-40, para. 65.
35. Ibid., 40, para. 65.
36. Douglas R. Burnett, Tara Davenport, and Robert C. Beckman, "Overview of the International Legal Regime Governing Submarine Cables," in Submarine Cables: The Handbook of Law and Policy, ed. D. R. Burnett, Robert C. Beckman, and Tara Davenport (Leiden: Martinus Nijhoff, 2014), 65.
37. "Territorial and Maritime Dispute (Nicaragua v. Colombia)," 674, para. 139.
38. Tanaka, The International Law of the Sea, 387 and 382-85.
39. "Pulp Mills on the River Uruguay (Argentina v. Uruguay)," Judgment, ICJ Rep. (2010, April 20): 14, 78, para. 193, quoting "Legality of the Threat or Use of Nuclear Weapons," Advisory Opinion, ICJ Rep. (1996): 241-42, para. 29.
40. "The MOX Plant Case (Ireland v. United Kingdom)," Provisional Measures, ITLOS sep. op. Judge Wolfrum ICJ Rep. (2001, December 3): 3.
41. "Case Concerning Land Reclamation by Singapore in and around the Straits of Johor (Malaysia v. Singapore)," Provisional Measures, ITLOS order, ICJ Rep. (2003, October 8): para. 92, quoting the MOX Plant Case, Order of December 3, 2001, para. 82. The duty to cooperate is stated in Article 197 of the LOS Convention.
42. "Pulp Mills on the River Uruguay (Argentina v. Uruguay)," 14, 83, para. 204 (20 April).
43. Judge Laing, "Southern Bluefin Tuna Cases (New Zealand v. Japan; Australia v. Japan)," Provisional Measures, ITLOS, sep. op. ICJ Rep. (1999, August 27): para. 16 and note 6; "The MOX Plant Case (Ireland v. United Kingdom)."
44. Churchill and Lowe, The Law of the Sea, 369.
45. Ibid., 355.
46. Ibid., 351.
47. Ibid., 352-53.
48. Tanaka, The International Law of the Sea, 260-61.
49. Ibid., 264 and 266.
50. Ibid., 264.

51. Ibid., 266.
52. "Final Report of the ILA Committee on Coastal State Jurisdiction Relating to Marine Pollution," Conclusion No. 2, in International Law Association, "Final Report of the Committee," 475 and 478-81.
53. U.S. State Department telegram, 28 February 1989, excerpted in Digest of U.S. Practice in International Law, 1989-1990, 478.
54. Robin Rolf Churchill and Alan Vaughan Lowe, The Law of the Sea, 3rd ed. (Manchester: Manchester University Press, 1988): 409.

Conclusion

1. Kammerhofer, J. Uncertainty in International Law: A Kelsenian Perspective. London: Routledge, 2011, 59-80.
2. Schlütter, B. Developments in Customary International Law: Theory and the Practice of the International Court of Justice and the International Ad Hoc Criminal Tribunals for Rwanda and Yugoslavia. Leiden: Martinus Nijhoff Publishers, 2010, 15-33.
3. Alvarez, J.E. International Organizations as Law-makers. Oxford: Oxford University Press, 2005, 143-182; see also Boyle, A. and Chinkin, C. The Making of International Law. Oxford: Oxford University Press, 2007, 116-120.
4. D'Amato, A. The Concept of Custom in International Law. Ithaca: Cornell University Press, 1971, 74-97.
5. International Court of Justice (1986). Case Concerning Military and Paramilitary Activities in and Against Nicaragua (Nicaragua v. United States of America), ICJ Reports 1986, para. 186.
6. Koh, H.H. "Why Do Nations Obey International Law?" Yale Law Journal 106, no. 8 (1997): 2599-2659.
7. Goldsmith, J.L. and Posner, E.A. The Limits of International Law. Oxford: Oxford University Press, 2005, 3-10.
8. Mendelson, M. "The Formation of Customary International Law," Recueil des Cours 272 (1998): 155-410.
9. Treves, T. "Customary International Law," in The Max Planck Encyclopedia of Public International Law, ed. R. Wolfrum. Oxford: Oxford University Press, 2006, 937-957.

Bibliography

Books

Abbott, Kenneth, et al. International Organizations as Law-Makers. Oxford: Oxford University Press, 2006.

Aron, Raymond. Paix et guerre entre les Nations. Paris: Calmann-Lévy, 1962.

Bedjaoui, Mohammed. International Law: Achievement and Prospects. Dordrecht: Martinus Nijhoff Publishers, 1991.

Besson, Samantha. The Morality of Conflict: Reasonable Disagreement and the Law. Oxford: Hart Publishing, 2005. https://doi.org/10.5040/9781472563491

Bonfils, Henry. Manuel de Droit International Public. 8th ed. Paris: Arthur Rousseau, 1914.

Brierly, J.L. The Basis of Obligation in International Law. Oxford: Clarendon Press, 1958.

Brownlie, Ian. Principles of Public International Law. 8th ed. Oxford: Oxford University Press, 1990.

Brunnée, Jutta, and Stephen J. Toope. Legitimacy and Legality in International Law: An Interactional Account. Cambridge: Cambridge University Press, 2010. https://doi.org/10.1017/CBO9780511781261

Buchanan, Allen. Justice, Legitimacy, and Self-Determination: Moral Foundations for International Law. Oxford: Oxford University Press, 2003. https://doi.org/10.1093/0198295359.001.0001

Bull, Hedley. The Anarchical Society. London: Macmillan, 1977. https://doi.org/10.1007/978-1-349-24028-9

Byers, Michael. Custom, Power and the Power of Rules: International Relations and Customary International Law. Cambridge: Cambridge University Press, 1999. https://doi.org/10.1017/CBO9780511491269

Cheng, Bin. General Principles of Law as Applied by International Courts and Tribunals. London: Stevens & Sons, 1954.

D'Amato, Anthony. The Concept of Custom in International Law. Ithaca: Cornell University Press, 1971.

Dworkin, Ronald. Taking Rights Seriously. Cambridge, MA: Harvard University Press, 1977.

Articles

Akehurst, Michael. "Custom as a Source of International Law." British Yearbook of International Law 47, no. 1 (1974): 1-53. https://doi.org/10.1093/bybil/47.1.1

Alter, Karen J. "Delegation to International Courts: Self-Binding vs. Other-Binding Delegation." Law and Contemporary Problems 71, no. 1 (2008): 37-76.

Axelrod, Robert, and Robert O. Keohane. "Achieving Cooperation under Anarchy: Strategies and Institutions." World Politics 38, no. 1 (1985): 226-254. https://doi.org/10.2307/2010357

Besson, Samantha. "State Consent and Disagreement in International Law-Making." Leiden Journal of International Law 29, no. 2 (2016): 289-313. https://doi.org/10.1017/S0922156516000030

Bodansky, Daniel. "The Legitimacy of International Governance: A Coming Challenge for International Environmental Law?" American Journal of International Law 93, no. 3 (1999): 596-624. https://doi.org/10.2307/2555262

Bradley, Curtis A. "The Juvenile Death Penalty and International Law." Duke Law Journal 52, no. 3 (2002): 485-557. https://doi.org/10.2307/1373162

Bradley, Curtis A., and Mitu Gulati. "Withdrawing from International Custom." Yale Law Journal 120, no. 2 (2010): 202-275.

Charney, Jonathan I. "The Persistent Objector Rule and the Development of Customary International Law." British Yearbook of International Law 56, no. 1 (1985): 1-24. https://doi.org/10.1093/bybil/56.1.1

International Documents

Advisory Committee of Jurists. Documents Presented to the Committee Relating to Existing Plans for the Establishment of a Permanent Court of International Justice. The Hague: Permanent Court of International Justice, 1920.

Advisory Committee of Jurists. Process-Verbaux of the Proceedings of the Advisory Committee of Jurists, July 16th-July 24th, with annexes. The Hague: Permanent Court of International Justice, 1920.

Charter of the United Nations. June 26, 1945. 1 U.N.T.S. XVI.

Committee on Formation of Customary (General) International Law. "Final Report of the Committee: Statement of Principles Applicable to the Formation of General Customary International Law." International Law Association, London Conference, 2000.

Council of Europe. Publication of Digests of State Practice in the Field of Public International Law. Strasbourg: Council of Europe, 1970.

Declaration on Principles of International Law concerning Friendly Relations and Co-operation among States in accordance with the Charter of the United Nations. G.A. Res. 2625 (XXV), October 24, 1970.

Documents of the United Nations Conference on International Organizations. United Nations Committee of Jurists, UN Information Organizations, vol. XIV. San Francisco: United Nations, 1945.

Draft Articles on Responsibility of States for Internationally Wrongful Acts with Commentaries. Yearbook of the International Law Commission 2001, vol. II, Part Two. U.N. Doc. A/56/10.

Draft Conclusions on the Identification of Customary International Law. Yearbook of the International Law Commission 2018, vol. II, Part Two. U.N. Doc. A/73/10.

International Law Commission. Fourth Report on the Law of Treaties by Gerald Fitzmaurice, Special Rapporteur. Yearbook of the International Law Commission 1959, vol. II. U.N. Doc. A/CN.4/120.

League of Nations. Committee of Jurists on the Statute of the Permanent Court of International Justice, Minutes of the Session held at Geneva (Final Report). Geneva: League of Nations, 1929.

League of Nations. Permanent Court of International Justice, Documents Concerning the Action Taken by the Council of the League of Nations under Article 14 of the Covenant. Geneva: League of Nations, 1921.

Rome Statute of the International Criminal Court. July 17, 1998. 2187 U.N.T.S. 3.

United Nations Charter. June 26, 1945. 1 U.N.T.S. XVI.

United Nations Conference on the Law of Treaties. Official Records, First Session, Meetings of the Committee of the Whole. Vienna: United Nations, 1969.

United Nations Convention on the Law of the Sea. December 10, 1982. 1833 U.N.T.S. 3.

Vienna Convention on Diplomatic Relations. April 18, 1961. 500 U.N.T.S. 95.

Vienna Convention on the Law of Treaties. May 23, 1969. 1155 U.N.T.S. 331.

Ways and Means of Making the Evidence of Customary International Law More Readily Available. Memorandum submitted by the Secretary-General. U.N. Doc. A/CN.4/6, 1949.

Yearbook of the International Law Commission. New York: United Nations, 1950-1976.

Index

A

Acquiescence, 25, 61, 95, 109, 117, 153, 159
Adoption (of legal claims), 97, 111
Anarchy (in international system), (see Geo-political systems)
Antelope, The case, 145
Arbitration, 11, 147
Asylum case, 43, 51, 59, 69, 147, 155
Attributes (in state interactions), 87
Australia, practice of, 35, 115, 137, 139, 153, 157, 165
Autolimitation theory, 19, 135

B

Bilateral customs, 43
Brazil, practice of, 133

C

Canada, practice of, 77, 121
Case law, 33, 57
Chile, practice of, 97, 121
Chronological law, 25, 63
Claim-oriented perspective, 77
Claims (legal), 91, 93, 95, 97, 99, 101
Codification, 103
Collective will theory, 23
Committee of Jurists, 11, 133
Consent, state, 3, 15, 17, 19, 21, 23, 25, 27, 47, 55, 57, 59, 63, 95, 137, 139, 141, 145
  As barrier against domination, 27
  As protective shield, (see pages on Consent)
  Challenges to, (see pages on Consent)
  Merits of, (see pages on Consent)
  Need for, 15, 17
  Original, 55, 57
  Relationship to treaties, (see Treaties)
  Theoretical framework of, 19, 23
Continental Shelf cases, 45, 83, 97, 117, 121, 123, 143, 147, 153, 155, 161, 165
Continuity (in state practice), 9, 53
Corfu Channel case, 121
Custom, 7-125 (passim)
  Bilateral, 43
  General, 43, 45, 47, 49, 61, 79, 117, 145, 161
  Regional, 43, 69
  Universal, 43, 49
Customary international law, 7-125 (passim)
  Definition of, (throughout main chapters)
  Development of, 103-125
  Formation and objection, 49-63
  Identification of, (throughout main chapters)
  Relationship to EEZ, 115-125

D

Decentralized interactions, 3
Delimitation, maritime, 51, 53, 95, 117, 121, 123, 153
Diplomatic protests, 39, 99

E

Effectiveness, concept of, 41, 99, 137, 149
Evolutionary principle, 55, 75, 89
Exclusive Economic Zone (EEZ), 115, 121, 123, 157, 159, 161

Development of, 115-125
National practice of, 119, 121
Recognition of, 117
Rights of coastal states in, (see EEZ main entry)
Scope of concept in customary law, 115-125

F

Falkland Islands, 87, 101
Fisheries case, 41, 49, 51, 53, 59, 61, 67, 93, 95, 101, 115, 117, 119, 121, 141, 143, 147, 149, 151, 153, 159
France, practice of, 61, 133, 151, 153

G

General acquiescence, 61
General custom, 43, 45, 47, 49, 61, 79, 117, 145, 161
General principles of law, 7, 37, 143
Great Britain, practice of, 95
Gulf of Maine case, 39, 51, 105, 121

H

High seas, 47, 115, 121, 123, 125, 161, 163
Historical background (of Article 38), (see Committee of Jurists)
Hudson, Manley O., 43, 155

I

Individual consistency, 51
International Court of Justice (ICJ), 11, 143
International Law Association, 161
International Law Commission, 25, 35, 45, 81, 103, 107, 111, 137, 141, 143, 149, 151, 161
International organizations, 11, 33, 107, 109
Intertemporal law, 101
Italy, practice of, 133

J

Japan, practice of, 133, 165
Joint Declarations, 35
Jus cogens, 3, 21, 23, 45, 47, 49, 57, 61, 83, 133, 143, 145
Jus dispositivium, 93

L

Landlocked states, 161
Lex specialis derogat legi generali, 143
Lotus case, 67, 141, 155

M

Marine environmental protection, 127
Marine pollution, 127
Maritime delimitation, 121
Minquiers and Ecrehos case, 41, 99

N

National digests, 139
Nicaragua case, 49, 67, 121, 123, 147, 153, 163, 165
North Sea Continental Shelf cases, 39, 45, 53, 95, 117, 121, 123, 143, 147, 149, 151, 153, 155
Nottebohm case, 41, 43, 67
Nuclear Tests case, 35, 153

O

Opinio juris, 15, 23, 25, 39, 67, 75, 77, 79, 81, 83, 107, 109, 117, 155
As an element of customary law, (see Opinio juris main entry)
As belief in legal duty/obligation, (see Opinio juris main entry)
Relationship to state practice, (see State practice)

P

Paquete Habana case, 55, 145
Persistent objector, 53, 55, 57, 61, 63, 145, 147
  Doctrine of, 53-63
  Historical background, 53, 55
  Limitations of, (see Persistent objector main entry)
Physical assertion, 41
Political expediency, 71
Pre-existing rule school, 81

R

Recognition, 9, 39, 41, 93, 95, 97, 99, 117, 153
  Of legal claims, 93, 95, 97
Regional custom, 43, 69
Renunciation, 95, 153
Repetition (in state practice), 9, 53
Right of Passage case, 43, 53, 73, 147, 149, 151, 153
Rome Statute, 135
Rousseau, Jean-Jacques, 151

S

Security Council, 15, 103, 135, 147
Self-determination, 37, 101, 103
Social necessity, 79, 83
South Africa, practice of, 33, 61, 143
Sovereign equality, 3
Sovereignty, 21, 23, 47, 63, 95, 99, 101, 103, 125, 153, 159
State practice, 11, 31-63, 81, 105, 109, 115, 117, 119, 139, 151
  Analysis of, 33-41
  Continuity and repetition in, 9, 53
  Individual consistency, 51
  National digests of, 139
  Relationship to subjective element, (see Subjective element)
  Widespread and consistent, (see Widespread practice)
Subjective element, 25, 67-83, 147, 151
  Analysis of, 67-83
  Relationship to state practice, (see State practice)
Submarine cables, 125, 165
Sweden, practice of, 115, 153, 157

T

Temple of Preah Vihear case, 159
Territorial sea, 99, 115, 121, 127, 161, 163
Thirlway's perspective, 79
Treaties, 11, 21, 25, 27, 31, 35, 57, 61, 107, 121, 137, 141, 143, 145, 149, 159
  Customary international law and, (see Treaties main entry)
  Relationship to EEZ, 121
Truman Proclamation, 77, 101
Turkey, practice of, 161

U

Uniformity, 49, 51, 53, 105
United Kingdom, practice of, 61, 95, 121, 141, 143, 149, 151, 153, 165
United Nations, 11, 17, 67, 103, 109, 123, 135, 141, 147, 151, 153, 155, 157
United States, practice of, 31, 55, 67, 77, 87, 93, 97, 101, 115, 121, 125, 133, 139, 143, 147, 157, 161, 163
Universal custom, 43, 49
US Nationals in Morocco case, 43, 53

V

Venezuela, practice of, 11, 55, 161
Vienna Convention on the Law of Treaties, 3, 137, 143, 159

W

Widespread practice, 7, 9

www.ingramcontent.com/pod-product-compliance
Lightning Source LLC
LaVergne TN
LVHW020414220926
848484LV00018B/2573/J
* 9 7 9 8 8 8 1 9 0 4 2 4 1 *